LADIES...
If Your Horse Is Dead,
DISMOUNT!

CESARIO, INC.
Sarasota, Florida

About The Author

Lynn McDonald is the developer of the Hoofs Up! series of training videos and workshops, based on her humorous but effective metaphor of "How to recognize when you're on a dead horse." As CEO of the training firm Cesario, Inc., which she founded in 1993, she wrote, directed, and performed in the international training video, " Hoofs Up, Doc! Rx for Change," which has been released in the U.S. and China. She is a frequent guest speaker at national trade shows, universities, and organizational meetings. She lives with her husband in Sarasota, Florida.

Manufactured in the United States of America
Library of Congress Catalog Card Number: 2003093830
ISBN: 0-9741990-1-X
Book design and production by Cesario, Inc.
Graphic Design by Laura Taylor
Cover by Cathleen Shaw

McDonald, Lynn, 1954

Ladies... If Your Horse Is Dead, Dismount! A Simple and Profound
Philosophy About Why You Can When You Think You Can't – Second Edition, August,
2004
LCCN: 2003093830
ISBN: 0-9741990-1-X

CESARIO, INC.
1620 Main Street, Suite 11, Sarasota, Florida 34236
(941) 906-2098 • www.nodeadhorses.com

This book is dedicated to Aunt Julia

Acknowledgements

Although my name may appear on the cover of this book, it is the women who courageously gave of themselves by sharing their stories with me who deserve all the credit. I thank you all.

I am also very grateful to Carol Gaskin, my editor, who magically changed words without altering my writing style or the spirit of my book. You are without a doubt a writer's dream come true, and to say you are a talented woman would be an understatement. Thank you for bringing my book to life.

This book could have never made it to the finish line without the patience and encouragement of the horse that appears in the photo with me. Wearing the horse costume is my husband, Michael—a thoroughbred in every way. As always, he's been quiet, strong, and incredibly supportive. Thank you for believing in me and that this book would be a Triple Crown winner.

Table of Contents

Introduction

At one time or another, as women, we're all faced with circumstances over which we believe we have no control.

For instance, imagine you are in the Run for the Roses. You're mounted on a world-renowned thoroughbred. All wagers are on your horse, and he's sure to be a winner. While you're waiting at the starting gate, secure in the saddle, you glance at the other horses. Just as you thought, there's no competition.

The race is about to begin. Your adrenaline soars. You grab the reins and position yourself in a winning style. Suddenly you realize your feet are not dangling in the stirrups—they're dragging on the ground! You look down, and you can hardly believe your eyes. Your horse is dead!

What control do you have over this situation? What would you do?

A) Hold your position and hope no one notices.

B) Drag the horse across the finish line.

C) Give it mouth-to-mouth resuscitation.

D) Realize your horse is dead and dismount.

Did you find you wanted to choose more than one answer? So did all the women you're about to meet in this book. Like them, we've all tried to

(A), cling to a "dead" belief or behavior and hope our friends and family will overlook it; (B), drag a lifeless idea around with us long after it has served its purpose; and (C), tried to breathe life into a situation that's too stiff to respond and may even be starting to smell!

The dead horses you'll meet in this book are not our lovers, our financial woes, our health problems, our upbringing, or any of the things we blame for our troubles. A dead horse is a mindset—a habit of thought that causes us to act against our own best interests. A dead horse is a mindset we need to let go of, so we can grow and prosper.

Each one of these brave women's stories will empower you to recognize the places you feel stuck in your own life and to dismount your own dead horses—to choose answer D!

What happens then? Like the ladies you will meet in this book, you trade in that old, dead horse for a strong, energetic thoroughbred that will carry you to your goal.

CHAPTER ONE

Hoofs Up!

Why did I write this book? That's a question I can only answer by telling you about an amazing woman who I called Aunt Julia. My Aunt Julia was more like a grandmother to me than an aunt, and she motivated me to write this book when I was just seven years old.

To me, Aunt Julia was the smartest woman in the world, even though she only completed the sixth grade. She had all the answers to my questions, and she was always right! She was a feisty Italian woman on the short side. . . .a big woman—no, make that a large woman—with gray, wiry hair, forearms like Popeye's, and a bosom that looked like two moons over Miami. When she hugged you, you prayed you wouldn't suffocate. There was nothing more comforting than her hugs, unless you counted her words of wisdom. Till this day, I can recall her low-toned voice speaking in broken English, as she would give advice like, "If an opportunity doesn't knock, you gotta ringa the doorbell."

At seven, I had no idea what she was talking about. Today as a business-woman, her advice makes perfect sense. Don't just wait for chances to arrive at your front door; go out, network, ring doorbells.

One other favorite word of advice she gave me was, "If your feet are firmly planted on the floor, how are you going to get your pants on?" I use this tidbit of advice every day in business. Such a simple and yet powerful message, don't you think? Don't just stand there, take a risk, even knowing you might lose your balance and fall. What the heck? You can always get back up. Otherwise you'll ask yourself for the rest of your life, "What if I had done this, or what if I had done that?"

I'll never have to ask, "What if?" because Aunt Julia taught me to be a risk-taker and showed me that all things are possible.

Take this book. Most people would have bet the farm that I would never be able to write it, because I have dyslexia. As a child, I was a very poor student. I struggled to get Ds and Cs. When I was in the fourth grade, I was placed in the ungraded room. That was the class the whole school knew as the "stupid" kids, or worse, the "retarded" room. If you had any doubt that you belonged in the ungraded room, it was totally destroyed when you were put into the reading group named the "Turtles."

School, as you can imagine, wasn't a place I liked to go. Within one year I was promoted to a regular class. I had no physical or mental indication of being (as they called it in the sixties) retarded, so I was given a "social" promotion. No one had a clue what dyslexia was back then, at least in my school. As a matter of fact, I struggled all the way through school and was never diagnosed with dyslexia until I was in my late thirties.

Dyslexia didn't stop me from becoming a successful businesswoman, though, because no matter what disability I had or how my intelligence was labeled, I felt that I could do anything I put my mind to. That was the greatest lesson Aunt Julia taught me.

I remember the day I learned that lesson. It was 3:30 on a Friday after noon. I came home from school clutching a crumpled sheet of paper that had a big red zero written on it. I opened the front door with tears running down my face. Aunt Julia was standing on the other side, and I ran into her arms sobbing, saying, "I'm stupid! I can't spell. All I can get is a big fat zero."

Auntie gently pushed me away from her and looked me in the eyes. "You, come-a with me," she said. She grabbed my hand and headed toward the parlor. When we reached the threshold of the door, she tugged on my hand and said, "Jump-a. Jump-a. You, jump over that doorway and run-a to the back of-a the room and come-a back."

Remember, Aunt Julia was a formidable woman, and if she said "Jump," you didn't ask questions.

I jumped over the threshold and ran to the end of the parlor and back. "See?" she said. "You jumped over your dead horse named 'I can't' and you mounted a thoroughbred named 'I can.' Don't you ever, ever think again that you can't do anything you put your mind to."

From that day on I became one smart kid. I looked at things differently. I knew I could spell. I just spelled the same word three different ways. Can you do that? That's pretty smart if you ask me.

That was the beginning, over forty years ago, of how I came up with the concept for this book. Today I realize that the threshold I jumped over represented a dead horse, a mindset I had programmed to say "I can't." I was the only one who could dismount that dead horse and jump on a thoroughbred, a new mindset that asks, "What if?" "Why not?" followed by, "Let's try."

Whenever I hear someone say "I can't," I smile and instantly recall Auntie Julia and the very day I learned the lesson of my life—the day I mounted my first thoroughbred and looked behind me, imagining a dead horse on its back with all four hoofs facing the ceiling.

"Hoofs up!" Now wouldn't that be a great comeback when someone gives you an excuse, like "I can't," or "Why change now? I have been doing it this way for years." Or how about this one? "It's not my job." Imagine looking that friend, family member, or co-worker straight in the eye, smiling, and saying, "Hoofs up with that!"

Today, at forty-eight, I'm the CEO of CESARIO Inc., a training and development company. I travel as a motivational speaker and conduct workshops for public, private, and non-profit organizations on my "Hoofs Up!" philosophy. I share Auntie Julia's words of wisdom and the true stories in this book about remarkable women from all walks of life who dismounted dead horses and saddled up thoroughbreds.

I know this book will give you confidence and encourage you to believe that you can do anything. Don't just take my word for it—Auntie Julia said so!

CHAPTER TWO

Men Aren't Dead Horses

Where is she? I hope I got the time right. She did say eight o'clock at the coffee shop, didn't she?

I was sitting in front of a café, talking to myself and looking at my watch, which read eight-thirty. As I was about to leave, I spotted a frazzled, plump woman hurrying across the street waving her hands high in the air. "Yoo-hoo," she yelled. "It's me, Mary Ann. Don't go."

Huffing and breathless, she reached the table, pulled out a chair, and plopped down. "Sorry I'm late. That's the story of my life."

She was certainly right. It was the story of her life. I soon learned that Mary Ann had been late for a lot more than just meeting me.

A mutual friend had suggested to Mary Ann that she and I get together to chair a community fundraiser. Over a cup of coffee, we discussed the possibility of working together on the project. The conversation quickly switched gears, however, from the fundraiser to her personal life. It was a vivid conversation that I still remember quite clearly.

Mary Ann told me she was divorced and that her ex-husband was a louse. "He won't pay me child support for our son," she said as her eyes filled with tears. To top it off, she said she had a great career as a sales consultant that suffered because she had to cope with the emotional trauma of the divorce each and every day.

Mary Ann talked for two hours about her personal situation. Over the next two months, we met almost weekly to work on our fundraiser project. Every time we met, our time together was totally consumed by discussions of her divorce. I really felt sorry for her. I couldn't imagine being in her shoes for one day. I just sat and listened, hoping I could do something to take her pain away. I couldn't help but think how difficult life must be for her, alone with a little child and struggling without child support. I can still hear her soft, tired voice saying, "He doesn't even buy toys for our son, and he never comes to visit."

The day before the big fundraiser, Mary Ann and I had our last meeting to tie up loose ends. Once more our conversation quickly shifted to her divorce. For the first time, I interrupted Mary Ann and asked her how long it had been since she got divorced.

"Fifteen years," she answered.

I thought I was going to fall off my chair! I found it incredible to think that Mary Ann had been dragging around a dead horse for a third of her life. That dead horse wasn't her ex-husband. She spent every day of her life weighed down by her very own habitual mindset. Mary Ann wasn't able to enjoy her life or move on to new and exciting things because of the powerful attachment she had to her dead horse named Blame. Instead of focusing on her wonderful job, her fabulous son—who, it turned out, had already graduated from college—she continued to whine, complain, and blame her ex-husband for her misery. She was crediting a man she hadn't even seen for fourteen years for everything that went wrong in her life on a daily basis!

After returning home from that meeting with Mary Ann, all I could think about was the fact that she had never once even remotely recognized that she was riding a dead horse—and getting nowhere fast.

The following week during a presentation to a group of teachers at a private school, I shared Mary Ann's story in an effort to make the point that you can't dismount a dead horse until you first recognize you're on one.

Several months passed, and I had all but forgotten about Mary Ann until my husband and I went to a garden shop early one Saturday morning. We were looking for some plants to put in a butterfly garden in our back yard. We had found just what we were looking for and begun to fill the shopping cart when I heard a voice yelling, "Hey, lady! Hey, lady!"

My first thought was that there must be a TV in the store playing an old Jerry Lewis movie. That was until the voice grew extremely loud and close to me. I turned toward the voice and was startled by a finger poking about two inches from my nose.

I stepped back as the tall woman the finger was attached to said, "Hey, lady...lady! I can't remember your name, but I have to thank you. You changed my life. I was one of the teachers at your seminar about dead horses. I am divorced, and I was so mad at my ex-husband for not visiting my son and doing things with him or taking him places on the weekend. Then you came along, and at that seminar I recognized that I was on a dead horse. I climbed right down, and now instead of spending my time being mad and complaining about my ex-husband, I spend my energy taking my son to all the places I wanted my ex-husband to take him. You really changed my life. Thank you."

What could I say? I was speechless, and so was my husband. As she walked away, however, my husband grinned broadly and said, "See? You really do have the ability to help change people's lives. You have to write a book."

I replied, "You're right. And I know just what I will title it: *Ladies, If Your Horse Is Dead, Dismount!*"

Hey, lady! Lady! I don't know your name either, but if you're reading this book, I sure want to thank you, because you changed my life, too, and hopefully the lives of many other women who will read this book.

CHAPTER THREE

Sitting Comfortably in the Saddle of a Dead Horse

Thirty-eight years. That's how long it took me to realize that Auntie Julia's lesson about dismounting a dead horse could change anyone's destiny. There was one catch. You couldn't climb off a dead horse unless you could recognize what a dead horse was.

If I had to give you a picture-perfect example of a dead horse, I'd have to take you back to the first time I met my husband. Here's how the day began. It was early Saturday morning, and I had just booked a motivational speaking engagement. While hanging up the phone, I glanced down at my calendar, only to realize I was twenty minutes late for my next appointment—the one that was going to change my life.

I dressed in a hurry, ran out the door, and I swear, I ended up stopping at every red light under the sun. Most people don't like red lights. I look at them as a gift—a few short seconds to reflect on life's events. As I approached the last red light, I could see the Midland Building to my right—the building where I had an appointment with an attorney.

While waiting for the light to change, I found myself thinking about the seven-year relationship I was in. My boyfriend was supposed to go with me to this appointment, and once again he was late...nothing new.

The light turned green, and I quickly pulled into the first available parking space. I grabbed my purse and hurried into the law office. By now you're probably thinking, What does this have to do with recognizing a dead horse? Here's where it becomes picture-perfect clear. Michael, the lawyer, greeted me with a warm smile and a handshake. When he let go of my hand, I felt as if I were floating on air. A little voice inside me said, "It's him, he's the one! Make plans, you're going to marry him!"

As I sat down, with what I know was the silliest-looking grin on my face, I heard a familiar voice call my name, jolting me back to reality.

"Lynn, sorry I'm late."

There before me stood my dead horse, my seven-year relationship. A relationship that was undeniably comfortable, but a relationship that was going nowhere and was never going to change.

Have you ever blurted out words before you realized they were coming out of your mouth? That's exactly what I did next. Without thinking I asked the attorney if he was married, and then went on to tell him I had some-one wonderful for him to meet. He smiled, and then my boyfriend asked, "Who?"

I mentally scrambled and threw out the name of the first person I could think of.

From that point on, the business part of the meeting went well. Michael incorporated Cesario, Inc., the business I named after my Aunt Julia. When the meeting was over, I packed up my things and walked out with my boyfriend.

On the way to the parking lot, the little voice came back in my head. It said, "Hey, what are you going to do about it?" In a split second I felt myself mentally hit the ground...as if I'd just fallen off a horse. The little voice inside my head was saying, "Glue factory—it's time to take this dead horse of a relationship to the glue factory, and don't look back!"

The little voice convinced me that I had many good reasons to dismount this relationship. I only wish that I had listened sooner. I wanted to get married; he did not. I wanted to have kids; he did not. I had dreams of the beautiful house with the white picket fence, a couple of kids, and two dogs running around. He definitely did not. My boyfriend had been happy living in the same apartment with the same furniture for more than twenty years. Are you getting the picture?

All that time I thought I was going to change him. I thought I could get him to want marriage, kids, and the whole kit and caboodle when twenty years couldn't change things in his life. He was perfectly happy, and I wasn't. I am sure I drove him crazy trying to change his life.

I realized that I had four choices. One, I could continue to stay on my dead horse, quietly hoping that someday my boyfriend would change his mind. Two, I could lug the dead horse around on my back and complain to all my friends about the relationship. Three, I could give the horse mouth-to-mouth resuscitation, trying to force life into a dead relationship. Or four, I could listen to the little voice inside my head that said, "Dismount that dead horse immediately, drag it to the glue factory, and find a thoroughbred named Possibility." I realized that I had no real choice but to dismount.

Ending the relationship that day was not as hard as I'd thought it would be. After all, I was the one who had dragged a dead horse behind me for seven years as I waited and waited for the relationship to change into the fairytale marriage I had dreamed of. My dead horse was a mindset I had programmed to believe that a comfortable relationship with someone who didn't want to get married would change if I just waited. I was so loyal to my dead horse that even when several "Prince Charmings" asked me out, I refused. I stayed with a dead horse called Settling for Less.

Until the day I met Michael, that is. Then the clock struck twelve and this Cinderella climbed off her old dead horse and mounted a new one named Possibility, as she watched her now ex-boyfriend head for the highway. I spun around, headed right back to Michael's office, and opened the door, riding proudly on a thoroughbred that whispered to me, "What if?" "Why not?" and "Let's give it a try."

At that moment, I felt as if Aunt Julia had come back as my fairy godmother to review the lesson about what a living horse says—the thoroughbred mindset.

"Did you forget something?" Michael asked.

"Yes, I forgot to ask you something. I have two tickets for the musical *Camelot*. Would you like to go?"

He said, "Sure."

I didn't really have tickets to *Camelot*, so when he said yes, I thought to myself, "God, please let the box office still have tickets left."

God came through, and what a night followed! *Camelot*, the original cast—Robert Goulet and Richard Harris—and to top it off, I was sitting with Michael.

I soon learned that Michael also had been dating someone for a few years in what had been a comfortable relationship. On our third date I asked him why he had broken off his relationship, and he answered, "She wanted to get married."

From the corner of my eye, I could see the rear end of my old dead horse backing into the room as that little voice in my head whispered, "You're not climbing back in that saddle again."

As much as I knew in my heart that Michael was the one, I wasn't willing to give up seven more years or even one more day sitting on a dead horse hoping and waiting for things to change. That's why I looked Michael in the eyes, knowing this could be the end of my dream relationship, and said, "I really like you, but maybe we shouldn't date, because to be honest, I do want to get married."

Mike smiled and replied, "You are not a very good listener, are you? I said I didn't want to marry *her!*"

From that day on I became a very good listener. Especially three months later when Michael said, "I do." This year we celebrated our ninth wedding anniversary.

Today my life is truly a fairy tale and my marriage is just what I had always imagined. Who knows what would have happened if I hadn't dismounted? My guess is nothing, absolutely nothing. This book would not have been written and, even worse, I would have never met the extraordinary women who are about to give you a glimpse of a time in their life when they recognized their dead horses and dismounted!

CHAPTER FOUR

Horsing Around at the Class Reunion

My Aunt Julia was an extremely honest and very blunt woman. When you asked for her opinion, you usually got more than you bargained for, including a reality check. That's why I couldn't lie to her when she asked me why I was sprawled on my bed in the middle of a bright, sunny Saturday while all my friends were out playing in front of the house.

I told her that my brother Butch was teasing me—that he'd said I was going to grow up to look just like her.

When Aunt Julia heard that she smiled and said, "Now, that's a bad thing? What part of me don't you want to look like?"

Even though I was young, I knew I could always dye the gray hair, and the two chin hairs I could pluck. But those moons over Miami! She could rest her arms on top of them, they were so enormous. I swear she could have thrown those breasts over her shoulders and tied them into a knot.

I answered, "Your twins." That's what I called them.

"Do you know what the twins are for?" she asked.

I shook my head no.

"When God made us, he gave man a brain, but he gave woman a brain and two storage compartments—one for all the extra knowledge we have, and one to store all the love we feel for our children."

She paused, sizing up my skeptical look. "You know how, when you can't find your homework, you ask your mother where it is, right? And when your dad can't find his keys, who does he ask? Mom, right? So you see, mothers have to think for the whole family, and that takes more brains than a man has. Remember when your mother was pregnant with your brother? Her twins got really big? That's because God had to give new mothers a place to store all the love that is growing for their new babies."

After that little chat with my aunt, I hoped for twins like hers because I now believed that women with large breasts were smart.

By age fifteen my body was developing new curves and bulges. My twins never got past a very modest size. I never thought much about my breasts; I just knew that they were two extra parts to wash in the shower, no different from my arms, legs, and face. But that all changed one morning when I was forty-seven.

That morning I switched from using a bar of soap to a liquid cleanser. While I lathered up, I felt a lump the size of a marble in my left breast. Of course, I thought the worst—the big "C" word. I went to my doctor. He felt it and didn't seem concerned. He said casually, "If it doesn't go away in a week or two, you might have to have it taken out." Then he recommended that I go home and put hot packs on my breast.

As I drove home I began to think that this was not a boil or a blemish that was going to come to a head. I really liked my gynecologist, but I felt a bit uncomfortable not being pro-active and getting a second opinion. So I called a radiologist friend who referred me to a surgeon he knew and respected.

I was scheduled to see the surgeon within one day, and three days after that appointment, I had a lumpectomy. The biopsy from the mass that was removed proved to be normal tissue. I had dodged a bullet, so to speak. Now I could go back to my normal routine and finish writing my book.

One week after my lumpectomy, I visited my throat doctor to ask about a weird feeling I had in my throat. My throat wasn't sore; it just felt funny when I swallowed, as if there was an extra small thing that didn't belong there.

My throat doctor proceeded with several tests over the next few weeks that revealed a node in my thyroid. He told me that the chances of my having thyroid cancer were slim to none, but I should have just one more test to make sure.

Thus, Robin entered my life. As I sat in the X-ray department of the hospital, I wasn't smiling or encouraging anyone as I usually did. I was scared to death, thinking I really hadn't dodged the bullet.

My husband was sitting to my right, and the woman next to him had a smile as wide as a rainbow. She was talking to an old man who was drinking an "X-ray milkshake," as I call it. The receptionist called the old man's name, and the joyful woman blurted out, "Don't forget to smile for the camera!"

God, was she happy. You would have thought she had won the lottery or that she was sitting on a feather or something. And to top it off, she was a chatterbox. I blocked out her voice with my thoughts of fear; but that only lasted a few minutes. That's when I overheard her tell the woman next to her not to worry—that she had just had a mastectomy and she'd also had reconstructive surgery.

"I never looked so good," she said enthusiastically, "and the best part is, I got a tummy tuck out of it. They took fat from my stomach to rebuild my bust."

For a split second I felt as if Aunt Julia was in the room, even though she had been gone for a few years. I felt her warm hug—not physically, but mentally, as she reminded me to admire a woman who could have chosen to sit on a dead horse named Pity, but instead was prancing on a thoroughbred named Will, the will to live.

Suddenly, at that one defining moment, I realized it was me who was on a dead horse: a horse named Fear. I knew what Aunt Julia would have told me to do right there and then—jump over the threshold and run across the room. Now that would have attracted some attention in the waiting room of the hospital—probably enough attention to admit me to the psych ward!

Instead of jumping and running, I introduced myself to Robin and asked her if we could get together. I told her a little bit about my book and that I would like to include her brave story.

One evening soon thereafter we enjoyed an after-dinner cup of coffee at my home as we sat comfortably in two oversized leather chairs in my library. I thought we looked like two little girls, all snuggled up in those big chairs as though we were at a pajama party.

Within a few minutes I felt as if I had known Robin all my life. Have you ever met someone like that? I knew that night that I had found a lifetime friend. Time seemed to pass so quickly as we talked about. . .well, you name it and we talked about it. But one conversation we had that night was about my experience attending my twentieth high school class reunion, and her excitement about her upcoming thirtieth class reunion.

"It's a funny thing, when you think about it," I told her. "You get an invitation in the mail for your class reunion, and the diet starts the next day. At least that's what I did. I felt like I was getting ready for my first date all over again."

I will never forget my twentieth class reunion. I confessed to Robin that I hardly recognized anyone until I glanced at his or her nametag. But by the end of that night, I was convinced that although time has a way of camouflaging our youth, it can never take away the soul—the inner beauty that made my friends so special in the first place.

I never thought I would meet anyone who was more excited than I had been about a class reunion. That is, until I met Robin.

"I can't wait to go to my thirty-year class reunion!" she told me. "And you'll never guess why!"

"Robin, would you like some more coffee?" I asked, looking forward to hearing the rest of her story.

"No thanks." She laughed. "At one time I would have killed for a second cup of coffee. I couldn't get enough of the stuff. I always had a cup in the morning before work. I worked in a bank that made coffee available, and I took advantage of that generous perk all day long. The cup of coffee I enjoyed most, though, was the one at night when my husband and I would sit quietly together, relax, and catch up on the day. Can you imagine liking coffee that much and then one day being told that it's off-limits to you—that you have to stop drinking immediately, cold turkey?"

I shook my head, no, but that's exactly what happened to Robin. She had gone to her doctor because her breasts felt sore, as if they were black and blue, though she knew she had no bruises. Her doctor assured her it was just caffeine. The doctor told her she had a very common condition, called cystic fibroid breasts.

"'A lot of women have it. Nothing to worry about. However, you should do away with any foods that have caffeine in them—coffee, tea, chocolate. Caffeine is known for causing tenderness in most women with cystic fibroid breasts.'"

Robin took her doctor's advice.

"Not only did I give up coffee, I actually threw away a half-full bag of my favorite candy, M&M's," she continued. "I don't know which was harder, giving up the coffee or the M&M's. Even though I followed the doctor's orders, six months later I still felt sore, so I went back.

"This time the doctor felt something she didn't like and immediately sent me to get a mammogram. After the test, I went right back to work. I knew if I buried myself in my work, I wouldn't have time to worry. That is, until the phone rang and it was the doctor's office. The results were in. My tests indicated that I had calcium deposits in my left breast.

"I took a deep breath and asked, 'So what's next?' My doctor said, 'We need a biopsy. I'll schedule a date for you as soon as possible.'

"I hung up the phone and once again buried myself in my work, and worried about money and paying bills—you know, the usual stuff. I had the biopsy. I was awake through the process. I felt as though I was in a Star Trek sick bay. They had me lie face down on a table and put my breast through a hole. The surgeon actually worked under the table. He numbed my breast and then took out the biopsy. It was a piece of cake. Afterwards, off to work I went. I convinced myself that I would have no time to worry if I kept busy."

Robin was more than busy. She held two jobs, her day job at the bank and a night job in a department store selling shoes. At lunchtime she would drive twenty minutes to visit her mom, who had bladder cancer.

I had a hunch that Robin worried more than she was letting on to me. I suspected she thought that if she stayed busy, it would all go away. As if she'd read my mind, Robin's voice turned from casual to serious.

"My doctor called with the results from my biopsy. I got lucky. It was benign. I hung up the phone, and once again my life was back to normal for several months. I kept up my busy schedule, with no time to waste. That is, until one morning, when I felt an oblong squishy mass in my left breast.

"It's no big deal, I thought. Probably just another one of those calcium deposits. I let it go for a few days, until I noticed my arm was sore. I told my husband, Ray, about the lump, and he said I'd better get it checked out. So off I went to the doctor's office, certain it was no big deal.

"But this time when the doctor examined my breast, her face indicated something was wrong, really wrong. She sent me for the usual tests, a mammogram and then an ultrasound. This time I was definitely worried. I went back to work and within one hour, the phone call came from my doctor.

"She told me I needed to see a surgeon, and she recommended one. I scheduled an appointment and had another biopsy within two days. This time the doctor's office did not call me with the results. Instead, they set an appointment for the next day.

"Ray stayed at my side the whole time. The surgeon couldn't have been any nicer. He greeted us and began by saying, 'I have bad news. I'm sorry to tell you, but you have breast cancer.' I sat numbly in shock. He talked a few minutes, but my mind switched to a dream sequence. It was as if he was Charlie Brown's teacher, you know, in the cartoon? She would talk, but all you'd hear was 'Wah, Wah, Wah.' All I heard was 'cancer.'

"My husband reached over and hugged me and said, 'Everything is going to be okay.'

"Before we left the office I did hear the doctor say, 'I recommend that you have a mastectomy. Time is important. We need to move fast. Go home and discuss it. I want to see you next week.'

"I didn't have a clue what to do next. Two little words had me frozen in my tracks: cancer and mastectomy. The only thing I could think about on the way home was how my husband would react to the way I was going to look. I loved him so much. I was afraid I would lose him. When we got home, we cried for three hours."

Robin was on a dead horse that she decided to dismount before wasting any more valuable time. That horse, named Pity, hung around and grazed a bit and was planning on staying for a while, but after three hours of crying and wallowing in self-pity, Robin mounted a new horse, a thoroughbred named Will—the will to live, to take charge—and off she went.

"My first stop was the bookstore. I read everything I could get my hands on. I wanted to be informed so I could feel in charge of my own destiny. I spent hours on the Internet, but most of the information was too general. I needed to know more.

"That's when I barged into my surgeon's office, just two days before the surgery. I sat and waited until he would talk to me. He was very kind and explained the whole procedure.

"Before talking to him I thought I was going to have my entire breast cut off and that I would have an indent, a hole in my chest. Boy, was I wrong. My surgeon, along with a plastic surgeon, spent seven hours in the operating room working on my left breast. And you know what? Turns out, I've never looked so good. The plastic surgeon actually gave me a tummy tuck to get some fat to rebuild my breast.

"Sure, I have a few scars, and it's difficult to look at sometimes in the shower. As for the recovery, it was not a breeze either. My husband nursed me back to health every step of the way. I went from flat to fluffy. I now have a size 'C' cup, and it's not an implant. It's actually my own flesh and fat from my tummy.

"Now my left breast is almost perfect. I have one more surgery to go on my left breast, and the plastic surgeon is also going to increase the size of my right breast so that I have a matching pair. For the first time in my life, I will actually have cleavage! That's why I can't wait to go to my thirty-year class reunion."

Robin was cancer free at her three-month check-up. She's looking forward to a long life ahead of her, with just one special cup of coffee at the end of each day with her husband. She enjoys work, but doesn't bury herself in it anymore just to keep busy. She has even made time in her busy schedule to take on one more job.

She volunteers at the Cancer Society, where she hopes to share her thoroughbred named Will with women who are ready to dismount a horse named Self-pity.

Robin, I know you will look like a modern-day version of Cinderella, cleavage and all. But remember: at the stroke of midnight your true friends will not see the physical you. They will see that you are the same soul with all the inner beauty that made them fall in love with you thirty years ago. You will always be my bosom buddy...the friend whose kind words and courage I can count on to give me a little push if I need it to get off a dead horse.

CHAPTER FIVE

Jockey in the Freezer

It just seems to happen. One day you hear yourself talking, and you think, "Wow! I sound just like my mother."

"One day" lasted thirty-eight years for Joann!

"At the age of thirty-eight, I did what I thought I would never be doing," she told me. "I walked down the aisle for the very first time. It's not that I didn't want to get married. It was just that my career and the time I spent traveling for work kept me busy and content."

Joann stopped and laughed, then said, "Okay, so you're not buying that, right? Here's the God's honest truth. I was not interested in marriage because of one other issue. I was petrified that if I got married, I would turn into—who else? My mother! Don't get me wrong, my mother had many wonderful traits."

Joann spent at least a half hour describing all the wonderful things that she loved about her mother, as if to defend her fear that she might turn into her mother if she married. Here's what I learned from Joann about her mother.

For starters, her whole family and all the neighbors called Joann's mother "Mama." She was a big, short, beautiful Italian woman who enjoyed cooking, cleaning, and lots of loving hugs. But Mama also loved something else—to incessantly nag her husband. Joann told me that she had made one promise to herself the night before her wedding. She vowed she would never become the nagging wife that her mother embodied every morning at the breakfast table and every evening at the dinner table.

Oh, heck, I may as well tell you everything I learned about Mama. She even nagged Joann's dad when family and friends were around. Joann had me in stitches when she said she was convinced that Mama probably nagged her father even while he was sleeping.

"Nagging aside," Joann continued, "my wedding day was phenomenal. Words could not describe my honeymoon, and the months to come would have been a dream for any bride. That is, until one day when I came home from work early and decided to tidy up the house a bit.

"While I was changing the sheets on our bed, I heard my voice echo Mama's for the first time. I found myself thinking, 'Just wait till he gets home. Is his arm broken or something? Can't he put his underwear in the hamper instead of playing basketball with it and missing the target?' In a split second after hearing myself sounding like my mother, I reaffirmed my decision not to become like my mother. So here's what I did instead.

"From that point on, every day when Larry missed the target and I spotted his jockeys on the floor, I would pick them up and chuckle as I put them in a Ziploc bag and then placed them in the freezer.

"Naturally, after two weeks or so, Larry started to run out of underwear. I was a good cook like my Mama, and I always had dinner ready for him when he got home from work. I could count the times that my husband went into the refrigerator on one hand.

"One night Larry asked me if we had any more Cookies & Cream, his favorite ice cream, left in the freezer. I told him that I wasn't sure as I reached for the ringing telephone.

"I was ending my phone conversation when he returned, and I'll never forget the look on his face. With the most dumbfounded wonder I have ever seen, he asked me, 'Did you know my jockeys are in the freezer?'

"Now keep this in mind. We lived in the country in the middle of no-where—a place where the nearest neighbors were three acres away. No one lived in our house but Larry, our two dogs, and me. So when I casually answered, 'No, I did not know your jockeys were in the freezer,' I can't imagine what Larry could have possibly thought.

"Till this day, ten years after we married, I don't think Larry has ever shared this story with anyone—not even his mother or business partner of twenty years. His mom thought I was a bit zany to begin with. She had her doubts about her son marrying someone with such a humorous and colorful personality. I'm sure he didn't want to hear her say, 'I told you so.'

"As for his business partner, I don't think any man would tell his friend, even a twenty-year friend, that he left his jockeys on the floor so his wife froze them until he figured it out.

"But figure it out he did. Since that day I have never seen a pair of Larry's jockeys on the floor again. As a matter of fact, he does his own laundry now. Who knows? Maybe he's afraid he will find his jockeys in the oven instead of the dryer.

"You know, now every time I hear my mother nag my dad, I chuckle and think to myself, that could be me and Larry on a day-to-day basis, if I hadn't changed my way of thinking by adding some humor to the situation."

I'll bet most of us can identify with Joann's dead horse. Have you ever experienced that one defining moment in your life when you said to yourself, "Oh, my God, I sound just like my mother"? That's not necessarily good or bad, but if your dead horse is a mindset like Joann's that has you programmed to believe that you will repeat your parents' failings, you may never get married.

The moral of this story? Sometimes a dead horse is an old nag! Joann thought she was fated to become like her mother and that she had no choice in the matter. At first her fear became a self-fulfilling prophecy, but she jumped right off her dead horse by changing the way she reacted to the situation. She turned a potential hazard in her marriage into something fun.

I'm sure that some day Joann's grandchildren will have fun telling her secret about the jockeys in the freezer to their children. Now, if we could only get Mama to read this book!

CHAPTER SIX

A Horse with No Sense of Time

Inhaling the aroma of my mother's gravy that was simmering in a big pot on the stove could only mean one thing—it was Sunday morning. Every Sunday as far back as I can remember, my mother would get up before the world to start cooking her sauce, or as most Italians who grew up in Rhode Island in an area called Federal Hill call it, "gravy".

Mom's gravy simmered on the stove for hours. The aroma reached far beyond the walls of our humble home right into the nostrils of our family and friends who didn't exactly live next door. The aroma of my mother's gravy must have been magical, because it seemed to summon Uncles Harry, Tommy, Bob, and Fred, along with Aunt Julia and several friends, to our house most Sundays.

My mother always put a plate filled with meatballs and a loaf of Italian bread on the counter next to her big pot of gravy. Before noon at least a half-dozen relatives and friends would stop by for a short visit, grab a meatball, and chat with Mom while she stirred the gravy.

My mother was a very hard-working woman. She cooked three meals a day for her family, kept the house spotless, and worked in a mill from 11 PM to 7 AM. Of course, as a young child I didn't think about how hard my mother's life must have been, but I did know she was tired. That's why I couldn't understand why my mother cooked for hours every

Sunday when she could have just bought TV dinners. Finally, forty years later, I understand.

Today mom is seventy-six, and she still cooks her gravy every Sunday. The pot she cooks in isn't as big. The plate of meatballs is now just a handful that fits on a saucer. The aroma still lingers beyond the walls of her home, but no one shows up anymore. Aunt Julia and most of Mom's brothers have passed on, and some just don't talk to each other. My brothers and sisters are busy with their own families, and I live in Florida.

Friends. . .well, what can I say? It seems as if no one has time to get together anymore. No one, that is, except for my friend Sandy, who insisted that I share her message with you—a simple, yet profound message about a dead horse so common that it's bound to hinder all of us.

"So many people take their friendships and all they have for granted," Sandy said with a tone of despair, followed by a deep pensive sigh. "Do you know what I mean?"

Before I could answer her question, Sandy slowly signaled me with her index finger to hold up a second. I stayed silent, watching her muster all of the strength her frail body could produce, then struggle to pull herself from a slouched, almost humped-back position to sit upright. I could see clearly that Sandy was not at all comfortable, even though she put on a smile and pretended she was pain free.

I waited patiently as if I had all the time in the world. I knew this was not going to be a walk in the park for either of us. Only a year and a half earlier, Sandy had sat on the same couch in my home, but she had looked so different then—a full-figured woman with long, flowing brown hair, eyes that smiled, and a laugh that brought a rainbow into your heart. Back then she was determined to focus and take charge of a movie production titled *Hoofs Up, Doc!*, a training video along the lines of this book that I developed for the corporate world.

The project seemed to be going nowhere in the hands of several friends. Although we all were extremely capable and competent in the production process, no one could hone in on a schedule, action plan, deadlines, and follow-up meetings. No one, that is, except Sandy, who was the wife of our animation and film editor. Sandy, who was the mother of a nineteen-year-old son and a seven-year-old daughter. . .Sandy, who was supposed to have been a silent visitor in the studio. . .Sandy, who I had come to love and admire for her determination, willpower, and drive. . .Sandy, who stood up and took charge to make sure that the job got done way before the deadline.

While our team often said we should get together soon, at the end of each meeting, Sandy would already have her pocket calendar in hand, prepared to set a date. As I reflect on our meetings, I now realize how magical her presence was. No matter how the day was going, she had a knack for bringing out the best in each of us. When we were dead tired, she never let us give up. Somehow she could always persuade us to work into the wee hours of the night with a positive but pushy attitude and, of course, a calendar in hand. I even affectionately nicknamed her Chief Nudge.

Six months into our film project, Sandy became obsessed with completing the project because, we found out, she was running out of time herself. Sandy was diagnosed with terminal melanoma.

All of a sudden, time took on a whole new meaning for all of us. Over the next year, Sandy became determined to fight a champion round and knock out the deadly form of skin cancer. We all knew if anyone could beat it,

Sandy could. But her closest friends could tell that behind her pleasant weekly e-mail updates on her progress, the melanoma was putting up a damn good fight, too.

Out of all the stories in this book, this one hit home for me the most. I hope it will touch and affect your life as it did mine, and make you realize the importance of time—perhaps the most precious commodity in the world, and the one that so many people just take for granted.

"Well, do you know what I mean? Are you listening to me, or are you daydreaming?"

Sandy startled me as she raised her voice.

"Sorry, daydreaming, I guess. Go on, tell me more."

She continued. "So many people take friends and all they have for granted, as if they have all the time in the world. News flash. We don't. Did you ever see an old high school friend in the grocery store and spend what seems to be an eternity catching up on everything, from how many kids you have to how your parents are? And just before ending the conversation, one of you says, 'Let's get together soon.'

"Several years later you're at a wedding, and there, sitting in front of you, is the same friend. You spend the rest of the evening catching up, talking about your grandkids, community events, even politics. By the end of the night, you two realize how much fun you have together, and once again you both promise, 'This time we really will get together soon.'

"Before you know it a decade has passed. You find yourself at the drugstore, once again catching up with your now very old friend. You share where to get the early bird specials, what ailments you have, and how much things have changed. Followed by, 'Oops, my prescription is ready. Hope to see you soon. We really need to get together.'

"So what's next? A funeral?" Sandy paused, and then said insistently, "We take friendships for granted. Somehow, we think that tomorrow, next week, next year is guaranteed. We think we have all the time in the world. Well, we don't."

At that point, her soft determined voice trailed off, and she sighed.

I need to tell you, I'm not a drinker. Had I been, this would have been the most sobering moment in my life. I excused myself as I held back the tears and went for a drink of water to compose myself. I couldn't help but think, How many people would relate to Sandy's dead horse named Let's Get Together?—a mindset we program to think we have all the time in the world.

The realization hit me like a ton of bricks. What I recognized, right then and there, was that this is a common dead horse we all know too well. Its true name is Procrastination. My visit with Sandy ended shortly after my drink of water, but I didn't dare say, "Let's get together."

Sandy was truly a champion fighter in her battle for life, but she was also right: we don't have all the time in the world. She fought hard and even defied the doctors' prognosis. Sandy hung on another six months after they told her she would die by Christmas.

When her time came, she was surrounded by friends and family. Others, I'm sad to say, didn't make it by in time to see her, and ended up saying good-bye at her funeral instead. I feel sorry for those people. And to this day, when I hear that phrase, "Let's get together soon," I don't procrastinate. I pull out my pocket calendar and pick a time, place, and date right there and then. Then I look up to the sky, smile, and thank God for Sandy's message.

Just like clockwork, every January I head out to the drugstore to get one of those free little pocket calendars in hopes of living the legacy of Sandy's message.

Don't take your friendships for granted. Dismount that dead horse named Procrastination and find time now to get together.

By the way, if you're ever in my neighborhood on a Sunday, you can find a pot of gravy simmering on my stove right next to a heaping plate of meatballs, waiting for my friends to stop by.

Mom, I finally figured out why you didn't serve TV dinners on Sunday no matter how tired you were. You knew how fast time would pass, taking family and friends away. You knew everyone had Sundays off and that your cooking would bring family and friends to our house, even if for only a few minutes. On Sundays, they all stopped and found time to get together.

CHAPTER SEVEN

The Horse on the First Floor

How many women do you know who win their first beauty pageant at age seventy-three? I know one—Sami Johns.

Sami became Ms. National Senior Citizen in 1999. I'll bet some people were surprised the night Sami won that title . . . surprised because she wasn't the typical beauty pageant contestant. You know, the twenty-four-inch waistline, perfect bust size, and bleached blonde hair. Nor was she your typical gray-haired, blue-eyed, sweet little grandmother who could be found baking cookies in her kitchen.

Rather, she's Lucille Ball, Carole Channing, and Carol Burnett all rolled into one, from her vivacious bright red—and I do mean red—hair, five-foot-tall plump stature, and her trademark wardrobe: all purple. Sami wore the color purple from head to toe, including her jumbo round purple rhinestone-rimmed glasses.

If you're thinking my description of Sami seems to portray a funny lady, she is. Sami is a standup comedienne. And get this—she got her first gig at the age of seventy!

I'm sure when the judges first met Sami they were blown away by two things—her vivacious stage presence and her active lifestyle. She was both the host of a TV show and the ring mistress of ceremonies for the Sarasota Circus, for which she also wore another hat as a member of the board of directors. Most importantly, Sami is best known for chairing countless fundraising functions for just about every charity in town.

In so many ways, Sami reminds me of my Aunt Julia. That's probably why I love having lunch with her every so often. Just like Aunt Julia, Sami can crack me up with just one facial expression. And just like Aunt Julia, she always greets you with a hug and a warm smile. Although Aunt Julia wasn't a standup comedienne by any means, she did act once in New York on the big stage, with her father when she was a child.

That was probably around the same time that Sami was acting in real life, playing the part of a young single mother who had so little money and so much pride—a long time ago.

As Sami tells it, "Back then I was working to support four children. I was a single mom in my thirties, living in borderline poverty. I worked three jobs and could barely manage to meet all my financial obligations. In the daytime, I worked in a factory soldering gadgets on an assembly line. In the evenings I waited on tables, and on weekends I found a job doing bookkeeping for a local business.

"I laugh when I think about how I got that bookkeeping job. I didn't know one thing about keeping books, but I sold the company on hiring me anyway. I needed the money for my children. When I left the job interview, I went straight to the bookstore, bought a book on how to keep books, and became a quick study.

"My day job was boring and depressing, but it kept food on the table. Most of the women I worked with were much older than me. It seemed as though they were perfectly content to think they'd be working in the factory for the rest of their lives. I couldn't understand that. I wanted more from life for my children and me.

"I will never forget the day that changed my life. I was working on the assembly line soldering gadgets one minute, and the next I was waking up in a hospital bed. I think I got sick from inhaling fumes from the lead solder. When I woke up in the hospital, the only thing I could think of was who had my purse. At the time, all I had to my name was a dollar and a quarter, and it was in my purse.

"I sat up in the bed as I thought to myself, 'I'm missing a day's pay. I won't get paid for today. How will I feed my children?' My own answer hit me like a ton of bricks. Welfare. I would have to go on welfare to survive.

"There was only one problem, and it was the same problem that had kept me off welfare all along...my father and my pride. My father was a well-known, well-respected man in town. I couldn't possibly go on welfare because I was worried I would embarrass him. And then there was my pride. You see, the woman who worked at the local welfare office was my high school classmate.

"I just couldn't ask for help from my dad because that, too, would hurt my pride. So I thought I had only one thing left to do. I got up out of bed, wearing only my underwear; I walked to the window and decided to jump.

"After all, I knew the kids would be much better off with my insurance money.

"That's when a little voice inside me said, 'Hey, dummy, you don't have any insurance.' To add insult to injury, I realized I was on the first floor.

"I backed away from the window as I swallowed my pride and made the phone call that changed my life. My high school classmate who worked at the welfare office couldn't get to my house any quicker than she did to help me. She was a real blessing."

Sami's dead horse was clearly named Pride. Her mindset stopped her from asking for help and kept her silent. Sami never complained to friends or relatives, no matter how bad things got. When Sami dismounted her dead horse by asking for help, things changed! Once she got on her feet, she moved to Florida, worked only one job, and became the wife of a wonderful man who treats her like his queen.

Sami might have been crowned Ms. Senior Citizen in 1999, but her friends recognized her royal qualities long before that night. Nowadays you just can't pick up the local newspapers without seeing Sami's smiling face coaxing the community to come to a fundraiser to help extend a hand to those with too much pride to ask.

When I finished writing this story about Sami, I read it aloud to her. Sami reacted with a big smile followed by, "Don't forget to add that when I registered for the Ms. Senior Citizen Pageant, I was the shortest, fattest, and the only one who wore glasses."

I smiled back and said, "Sami, when I grow up, I want to be just like you!"

She replied, "Me, too!"

CHAPTER EIGHT

A Mayor, a Saddle, and a Fishing Rod

Most people enjoy sleeping in on Sunday mornings, and I'm sure my husband would love to be one of those people. However, he is right by my side at 7 A.M. every Sunday, helping prepare breakfast for the homeless at a small church hall.

Out of all of the Sundays that we volunteered to help feed the homeless, one particular Sunday morning will stand out in my mind forever. It was the Sunday that Michael and I were at least twenty minutes late getting to the breakfast hall. When we arrived I was relieved to discover some new volunteers in the kitchen, because I knew that with their help, breakfast would be served right on time as usual.

When the church hall doors opened at 8 A.M., the attendance was almost double that morning. Somehow, the word must have gotten out that we were serving ham and eggs instead of our usual menu of dry cereals, muffins, coffee, and orange juice. I was amazed at how the new volunteers jumped right in and made a potentially chaotic morning seem as smooth as butter.

We all worked twice as fast and twice as hard that morning. When the rush was over and all had been served a hot breakfast, I knew I just had to have a cup of coffee to notify my brain that I was truly awake.

As I reached for a cup, I noticed one of the new volunteers, a short African American woman wearing jeans and a casual white top. She was standing in front of the kitchen sink filling a small white plastic bucket with water and some bleach. By the time I poured myself a much-needed cup of coffee, she had already put a hand towel into the bucket, wrung it out, and started wiping down all of the kitchen cabinets. Clearly she didn't mind rolling up her sleeves and getting dirty to help others.

Boy, was she fast and thorough. I couldn't believe my eyes. By the time I had taken a few sips of coffee, she had already emptied the trash, wiped down all the tables, and started washing dishes.

"Wow, where did she come from?" I blurted. I asked one of the other volunteers if he knew her name.

He stared at me incredulously and said, "Carolyn. You don't know her?"

"No, should I?" I responded.

He smiled broadly. "She's Carolyn Mason, our mayor."

I introduced myself to Carolyn and thanked her for helping us. Carolyn continued to volunteer every Sunday. Over the weeks to come, I got to know a lot more about Carolyn—perhaps a lot more than the towns-people who know her as the mayor. I learned that her soft yet powerful voice always carried an honest message. And I learned that Carolyn was a softhearted but strong and determined woman on a mission to make life easier and happier for those who needed a helping hand . . . as she had when she was only fourteen years old. That's how old Carolyn was when her mother died, leaving her and a two-year-old son behind.

Custody of Carolyn and her little brother became part of a battle between her two older sisters, one who lived in Connecticut and one who lived in Florida. After they duked it out, so to speak, the final decision allowed Carolyn to stay in Florida and to live with her oldest sister, who had a daughter just one month younger than Carolyn.

I learned one more thing about Carolyn—that she loves to fish and that she never gives her fish away. What she does give away is fishing lessons to anyone who wants to learn. Carolyn is a great fisherman. I think you will agree after you hear how she learned to fish herself.

"I was seventeen and a senior in high school when I got pregnant. I guess you could say I never had that talk with my mother about the facts of life, but I do remember one talk we did have. She told me to always remember, 'No one owes you a thing. If you want something, you have to work and work hard for it.' My older sister also told me something the day she found out I was pregnant. She told me that I was a disappointment. She said that she had had big plans for me, and then she threw me out of her house.

"There I was, seventeen, pregnant, with no place to go. My boyfriend turned to his grandmother for help. At the time, it just so happened that his grandmother had an empty apartment next door to her. I had nothing, and this wonderful woman took care of me. I dropped out of high school and was going to night school to get my GED. I actually graduated within weeks of my high school classmates.

"In my seventh month of pregnancy, my boyfriend's grandmother moved me into her house. She started plans to give us an elaborate wedding. The baby came, and the boyfriend left. He found a girlfriend, and I found depression.

"Now I was a seventeen-year-old mother, living with my ex-boyfriend's grandmother and a six-month-old child. I got so depressed, thinking I had nothing to live for, that I took a walk in the neighborhood, sat under a street light, and decided to swallow a full bottle of aspirins.

"I remember waking up in the hospital. I was lucky; the doctors were successful in pumping the excessive amount of aspirins out of my stomach. When I was released from the hospital, I moved back in with my sister.

"You know, my sister never said she was sorry for throwing me out, but later in life, I realized it was the best thing she could have done for me. It reminded me of what my mother taught me. No one owes you anything. You have to work hard for what you want. And that's just what I did—work hard. While living with my sister I held two jobs and took care of my baby.

"Ironically, one job was at the welfare office—a place where I could have easily been standing on the other side of the counter if it hadn't been for the memory of my mother's words: 'No one owes you a thing. If you want something, you have to work and work hard for it.'

"As the years passed by, I definitely could have taken the path of self-pity in my life, but instead I learned to take the negative and turn it into lifelong lessons that ended up building my character and helping me grow. I had three children and two failed marriages, all of which helped me become the person I am today—a fisherman. My life goal is to teach others in need to fish for themselves so they don't have to depend on others to give them fish.

"My sister probably doesn't know to this day how instrumental she was in teaching me to fish instead of giving me the fish. At seventeen, I was a poor black female. Today I'm liberated, self-educated, and the mayor of this great town; but I'm still black, a woman, and poor by most people's standards. I'm not embarrassed about any of that. I would only be embarrassed if I didn't help other people fish."

Something tells me Carolyn wasn't sitting alone under that street light the night she swallowed the bottle of aspirins. Beside her sat an ailing horse that kept muttering, "You have nothing to live for." When Carolyn's doctors saved her life, the ailing horse vanished just like that, leaving behind a saddle and an old fishing rod. In no time at all, Carolyn mounted a thoroughbred named Hope.

By the way, if you're ever looking for Carolyn and her horse, Hope, they can always be found somewhere in a part of town where most people won't go, teaching those in need to fish.

To this day, Carolyn is the only black female mayor in history to hold office in Sarasota, Florida. She is a mayor who works hard every day to get just what she needs for the people in her town. And yes, Carolyn really does like to fish!

Carolyn, you are without a doubt the world's greatest fisherman. Thank you for teaching the homeless and those in need to fish and cast their nets.

CHAPTER NINE

The "Bridal" Horse

"I'll have the fruit salad and a glass of water with lemon, please."

"Me, too," Ruth said in her charming South American accent.

I smiled at my companion, an attractive raven-haired woman wearing an elegant rose-colored silk blouse and a long flowered skirt that fit her well-proportioned body like a model. She scanned the menu, then looked up at me with bright, doelike eyes. "Cheesecake!" she said. "We're having salads for lunch, so I'll order cheesecake for dessert!"

While we waited for our salads to arrive, Ruth pulled out a photo of her six children and started telling me about them. She seemed to glow when she talked about the colleges they attended and how special each one was. The youngest was a boy. He looked about fifteen. When I pointed out that her daughters looked just like her, she smiled.

"Does your son resemble his dad?" I asked.

"Sort of," Ruth replied.

"Do you have a photo of your husband?"

"No!"

She started to explain, but just then the waiter placed our salads in front of us. Ruth hardly touched her food, she was so eager to share her story in hopes that it would help other women. As I started eating, Ruth began to speak.

"There I was on my wedding day, walking down the aisle in a simple, yet elegant pure white dress that took me one very long month to make. My parents were so proud. Their daughter, just nineteen, was about to marry a doctor—someone they thought would take care of their little girl for life. What more could a parent ask for?

"My mother had only one request on my wedding day. It was a bit unusual, I thought, but I always aim to please. So I said okay to having both my mother and my father walk me down the aisle, followed by my future husband, who was accompanied by his parents.

"You can't imagine how overwhelmed and unfamiliar I was with the grand scale of this event. Just one night before my wedding day, I was a college student sleeping in a twin bed in my dorm room. I liked living on campus. At the time, I had only two years left to graduate. I was also a devoted Christian who attended Bible study as much as I could between my part-time job and going to classes.

"I'm sure my religious interest had a lot to do with my upbringing. My dad was a Presbyterian minister. Both my parents were very well educated. In fact, they both received their doctorates in the United States and then returned to their homeland, Colombia. I stayed in the U.S. with one goal, to get my teaching degree.

"Juan, the man I was about to marry, was Mexican. His parents planned the whole wedding. I mean everything, right down to the smallest detail. They selected the hall, the entertainment, and even my wedding date. I was told not to worry about anything except for getting my wedding dress.

"I wrote to my mother in Colombia and asked if she could send me the money to buy a sewing machine so I could make my wedding dress—in between going to classes, my job, and Bible studies.

"My sister and two brothers were excited about flying to America for my wedding, along with about twenty other family members. I envisioned a small quaint wedding, with about thirty-five people and my dad performing the ceremony.

"That was until I opened the church doors! I had no idea that the Mexican wedding that was being planned for me by Juan's parents would be anything like this. The thirty-five guests I had imagined turned out to be more like five hundred thirty-five!

"In the procession before me were six Mexican couples, all dressed to kill. The women's dresses must have cost a fortune, especially compared to the simple straight A-line dress I was wearing. There were six Maids of Honor, a mariachi band, and a ten-piece band that was hired for the reception dinner."

Ruth sighed, and her eyes took on a faraway look.

"The music started, and I walked down the aisle followed by what looked liked a parade. When we turned toward the altar, I looked behind me, stared straight into the eyes of the man who was about to become my husband, and thought, 'I can't believe I'm marrying this man.'

"For the first time it really hit me. I thought, 'What am I doing? I'm not attracted to him in the least. He's overweight. We don't share the same culture or any of the same views on life. This can't be for real!' I felt like I was standing in the middle of a dream, but I couldn't wake up.

"The last few steps I took to the altar were the longest. I kept thinking, 'How can this be so bad?' One thing I knew for sure—there were no sparks between us. Maybe because of my religious beliefs, I felt guilty about premarital sex. 'Perhaps it will be totally different once he is my husband,' I thought. I hoped there would finally be fireworks on our wedding night.

"My parents thought he was a great catch, mainly because he was a doctor, so they knew he could provide a great life for me. Like most girls of my age and culture, I grew up believing my parents always knew what was best for me. Parents always know what's best for us, right?"

She grinned, and I rolled my eyes, but didn't interrupt.

"By now, you're probably wondering, did I say 'Yes'? Was I about to please my parents? As I said, I always aimed to please and make everyone happy, even at the expense of my own happiness. So yes, I said, 'Yes, I do,' in the faith that everything would change once Juan became my husband.

"It was late into the evening when the last guests left. I was ready for the fireworks to begin, but Juan had a different idea. He just wanted to open all the envelopes and count the money. So he did, and then he fell fast asleep.

Seven children later, I finally woke up from that nightmare, after two decades of sleeping next to a man I called my husband and only seeing fireworks on the Fourth of July—in the sky, of course. After twenty years of serving as a doctor's wife on community boards. . .twenty long and grueling years of attending functions with my husband, smiling and pretending to be happy, finally I woke up. And in that instant, it became more than obvious that I never loved my husband and I wasn't happy. I realized then that no matter how hard I tried, it was not going to get better."

Ruth waved a dismissive hand in the air. "So I left all the monetary things behind—the big house, the luxury car, and the high profile life of being a doctor's wife. I have very little now financially, but I'm the richest person in the world if you count happiness as wealth.

"Twenty years of being married to the wrong person taught me a valuable lesson. The lesson I learned is that once you're an adult, your gut feeling generally knows what's best for you—not your parents and not your friends.

"I now tell my children, 'Before you please anyone else, you must be true to yourself.' Today at the age of forty-two, I am starting my life over. I hope to reclaim the happiness that the nineteen-year-old girl I left behind on my wedding day deserves."

Like most of us, Ruth embraced a mindset as a child—a mindset that believed her parents would always know what was best for her. Understandably so; after all, our parents loved us, protected us, and even made our decisions for us—decisions like where we would live, where we would go to school, and what we would wear.

Our parents make these decisions for us until our journey begins, the same journey our parents took—the journey that takes us from childhood to adulthood. Our journey can only be described as like a ride on the Concorde. When we deplane as adults, we walk away knowing that we now have developed our own sense of what is best for us. Some of us call it a gut feeling, while others call it intuition. I refer to it as "dismounting an old mindset."

Understand, there is nothing wrong with embracing a mindset. But a mindset that never changes as time goes on will likely develop into a dead horse. Change is good!

If you still think your parents know what is best for you, you're probably dragging a dead horse behind you named Guilt—the same horse that Ruth dragged behind her down the aisle in hope of pleasing her parents. . .the same horse that Ruth hoped nobody would notice her sitting on for twenty years while she stayed in an unhappy marriage.

CHAPTER TEN

If Horses Had Wings

"I must have died and gone to heaven!" That's exactly what I thought as I looked at the woman who was sitting across from me in a pink Victorian wing-backed chair. She had the face of an angel, porcelain skin, twinkling blue eyes, and fluffy, pure white hair styled in a perfect French twist.

"Hello, I'm Angie. You must be Lynn?"

This came from a lilting voice as angelic as her appearance.

"Thank you for coming to see me," she continued. "My friend's daughter told me about you. She said you were writing a book that would help women, right?"

I smiled and nodded. "Yes, I am."

"What is the title of your book?" Angie asked.

"Ladies, If Your Horse is Dead—Dismount!"

Angie laughed. "Do you think you would be interested in an old woman's story? One I know will help a lot of women?"

"Certainly," I replied. "I'm all ears."

Angie smiled and looked to her right as she said "Hi" to two women shuffling slowly past us. One woman was using a walker, the other woman a cane.

"Those are my friends. They're really lovely ladies, you know. They live a few doors down from my room. The one with the cane, that's Suzie. She always saves me a seat for our Sunday services. Marlene is the one with the walker. She is eighty-eight and she still has a car, but her daughter keeps it for her because she can't see well enough to drive."

Angie seemed to enjoy small talk, but that stopped when she asked me, "Do you like to drive?"

I answered, "Yes, but not long distances."

Angie leaned forward as if she was going to tell me a secret and whispered, "I love to drive. Driving used to get me away from it all. In particular my husband. He was such an overbearing person who seemed to enjoy agitating me. I wouldn't let him rattle me; instead, I would head straight for the garage, get in my car, and take a long drive into the country."

She settled back comfortably in her chair and reminisced. "Driving was so relaxing to me. You know, I didn't drive till I was forty! I actually taught myself. I had two children late in life. I was thirty-seven, married for thirteen years, when I was blessed with my first child.

"My husband traveled every week. He was a salesman for a meat packing company, and later he sold corrugated boxes to manufacturers. While he was away I was stuck in the house with two beautiful boys, whom I treasured and adored so much. I wanted to share and expose them to the world. That's when I taught myself to drive.

"My children loved to take rides in the car, as much as I love to drive.

When my boys were very young, on rainy days it became a tradition to pile into the car, drive down the backcountry roads, and count the cows on the way into town to our local five and dime. When we got to the store the boys would each get a bag of popcorn. Till this day, I don't think it was the popcorn that really excited them. It was the ride in the car.

"On weekends, when their father was home, a ride in the car became more than getting popcorn—it was an escape. When Mick—that's my husband's name—came home after being gone for a week, he would act as though he was the king of the house, and the children his royal servants. 'His Royal Highness' insisted that he be waited on hand and foot."

Angie made a sweet little harrumphing noise. "For me it was actually easier to take care of two delightful children than one childish, bratty husband. I used to think I could bear with it because he was only home on weekends. Then he decided to become self-employed. He stayed in the same business, selling corrugated boxes. But he stopped traveling and worked out of the house.

"Mick just couldn't stand to be on the road not knowing where I was or what I was doing. He had to be in total control of everything. When he started working at home, I became much more than a wife and a mother. 'His Royal Highness' granted me a third job, as his 'Royal Personal Secretary.'

"I was a good wife and always supported my husband in any way I could—even though he was a royal pain in the butt. Often, nights, I would stay up working on his payables and receivables while he went out to his Kiwanis meetings.

"He had several very large accounts that he relied on, but after awhile he became complacent and didn't service any accounts in person. He would call his accounts and ask what they needed once a week. Eventually he stopped calling on his small accounts altogether. He said they weren't worth the bother. After all, he had the big accounts to rely on."

Angie shook her head in exasperation. "When it came to money matters, my husband was never much of a saver, but that didn't matter. Every year, he had to buy the biggest car on the lot, just to show off. I had no choice at all in the selection of our cars. My husband would pick up the car and show up in the driveway tooting his horn loud enough so the neighbors would look out of their windows.

"Mick was actually able to coast with those several large accounts for several years without his income changing—until the leadership changed in the companies he relied on. Sure, he still called once a week and asked for their orders, but the new regimes hadn't a clue who Mick was.

"I guess there is something to be said for nurturing relationships in person. Eventually he ended up losing the accounts. But, believe it or not, our financial situation didn't stop Mick from spending money. With no accounts and so much time now on his hands, he took up golf.

"Our savings account finally dwindled down to three hundred dollars. That's when, at the age of fifty-five, he decided to just retire. We had barely enough money to scrape by each month.

"By that time my two sons were off at college. How I love them! My sons were my whole life. Even though Mick was there, I always felt so alone, and worse than that, we were practically broke.

"I was fifty-five. Some would say that was over the hill, but that's when my life started. I stood up for myself and decided I could support myself. Actually, truth be known, I had no choice. I knew I had to do something before Mick put us in the poor house. That's when I enrolled myself in Real Estate school—of course, without Mick's blessings or support.

"It seemed as if overnight I became one of the top producers in the real estate office I worked in. I ended up selling real estate for twenty years. I was seventy-five when I stopped. I didn't retire. It was just that Mick had open-heart surgery, and I became his full-time nurse. He was actually happy, because this meant I had to stay home with him all the time and not leave the house to go to work. He never supported me in selling real estate. Well, he did come to all my open houses, but that was just to keep an eye on me. He was a jealous man.

"Nursing Mick back to health took a toll on my own health. He was really a handful. He never followed the doctor's orders. Can you believe he actually ate a half a pound of bacon and six eggs for lunch, just one week after open-heart surgery?

"He never had many friends because he was so self-centered. After twenty years of supporting Mick, I was tired and out of energy. I knew I was starting to get a little forgetful. I actually paid some of the same bills twice. It wasn't easy taking care of him, the household, and pretending to my children that everything was just fine.

"And I couldn't believe that once again, I was worried about money. I had saved over one hundred thousand dollars from my real estate sales. But after taking care of Mick and all his medications, I had only eight hundred dollars left in a savings account. We lived in a condo that was paid for, but there were still bills to pay. We ate at McDonald's, and hot dogs became a favorite dinner.

"My son, who lived in Florida, came to visit and insisted that we move close to him. I didn't know how I could pack everything and just move. Thank God, I didn't have to worry. My son and his wife took care of the whole thing.

"I sold our condo and was once again relieved to have some savings. Shortly after we moved to Florida, I fell and broke two bones. After rehab, my doctor recommended assisted living.

"Mick wanted nothing to do with it, but this time I was the one who needed help. It was amazing. Before we moved to Florida, Mick was like a zombie; I did everything for him. Now he was alert and doing well, and I took a turn for the worse.

"I was scared of living on my own, and worse, scared of living with Mick, who was back to being his overbearing self. I told Mick he had no choice in the matter. We were moving to assisted living. I looked forward to someone else cooking for me. Most of all, I wouldn't have to worry about paying bills at the end of each month.

"Once more my son and his wife helped us pack and move here. I loved making new lady friends. As for Mick, he found fault in every-one, as usual. We used to live together in that last room down the hall." She pointed.

"You don't live there anymore?" I asked.

"Well, Mick couldn't get along with anyone. He argued all the time. He would hold my hand every time we left our room. Most of the staff thought we were so in love. What they didn't know was it wasn't love at all; it was ownership. If Mick was mad at someone, he wanted me to be mad, too.

"I couldn't leave our room without Mick. He would yell at me and push me around. You've probably noticed by now I often did things later than most. I had children at thirty-seven and learned to drive at forty, not to mention real estate school at fifty-five. Well, now at eighty-two, I longed to have control of my life. I wanted to be number one, not second as I always was to Mick.

"So you know what I did?" She grinned blissfully. "I finally threw Mick out! He has his own room down that hall." She pointed in the opposite direction from her own room.

I guess I couldn't have looked more surprised. If I'd thought Ruth was late, Angie proved it was never too late to dismount a dead horse!

"He can't yell or tell me who to talk to anymore. I have a roommate, and she is a good friend. Lots of the ladies invite me to sit with them at dinner, and they always ask how I am. As you can see, I'm doing just fine, just fine."

Angie was one of the most gracious ladies I have ever met. She was right when she said she had a story that would help a lot of women—especially those who are wondering if it's too late to dismount a dead horse.

If Angie dismounted at eighty-two, it's proof that it's never too late to dismount a dead horse—even the one that convinced Angie for sixty years that she had no choice but to put up with Mick.

I can recall as though it was yesterday the first time I set my eyes on Angie. Truly, I thought I was seeing an angel sitting in front of me in her pink, wing-backed chair. At that time I was wrong, because Angie was very much alive and real.

Six months after I met her, however, Angie became a real angel.

The night I heard that Angie had passed on, I dreamt of her. In my dream Angie was sitting on a pure white thoroughbred in a pink satin saddle with stirrups made of pearls. The horse looked magical as it spread its angel-like wings and whisked Angie through the gates of heaven.

Such a beautiful dream, don't you think? And not too far from reality. After all, Angie did ride a white thoroughbred on earth, if even only for a short time. It was the same white thoroughbred that waited patiently through the years for Angie to dismount her dead horse named Fear. Angie, at age eighty-two, finally took the reins of that white thoroughbred on the day she moved into her own room.

The horse's name was Freedom. Need I say more?

CHAPTER ELEVEN

The Horse and the Garden Party

Twelve attorneys were focused on me as I said, "Good morning and welcome to the Legal Aid retreat. I'm Lynn McDonald, your facilitator for today."

I reviewed the day's agenda with the group, then kicked off the retreat by introducing the president of the board. After the president spoke, I introduced Audrey, whose topic was the future funding of Legal Aid.

In all my years of training and facilitating, I had never seen eyes like Audrey's. They were overflowing with passion and determination as she delivered her talk. As I listened to her forceful, yet subtle, presentation, I couldn't help but notice how all of the attorneys in the room seemed to be persuaded by her words. I had a gut feeling that behind those eyes was a story for every woman to hear.

At the end of the retreat I asked Audrey if she would be willing to share a story about her life for my book. I explained that I was writing about women who had embraced change and presented her with a brief introduction to the dead horse philosophy. She listened, smiled, and promised to check her schedule.

The next day I received an e-mail from Audrey that listed a few dates and times she was available to meet, followed by a short message that read, "If you don't find my story worthy, I'll understand."

Once again I had a feeling Audrey had a story, but now I sensed it wasn't just a story, it was the underlying reason for her impassioned advocacy of the need for funding for Legal Aid.

Audrey and I agreed to meet for breakfast early the next morning. Over breakfast I discovered that we had a lot in common, including the obvious—we were both of average height with brown hair and brown eyes. We would go unnoticed in a roomful of people—until we spoke, that is. The one dynamic trait we truly had in common was the ability to stand up and speak from our heart about what we truly believed in, as we encouraged others to partake in our cause.

We had both been raised in a second-generation Italian family with a strong work ethic. We laughed about the way our families never talked openly about most things. Everything seemed to be a secret—especially family problems or, God forbid, sex. We were both taught early on that what went on inside your house was not up for discussion anywhere but inside your house.

"When I went to college," Audrey told me, "I made two new friends, Sara and Peggy. They were like a breath of fresh air. The two of them talked openly about everything. The three of us became best friends in no time, and I became as comfortable as the two of them about discussing anything, including my most personal thoughts. Even when we went to the ladies' room together, no one was left out of a conversation. I can remember Peggy sitting on the toilet, holding the stall door open so she wouldn't miss out on any of our conversations!

"This was totally new for me. It would have never happened in my house.

I loved and treasured my new friendships and enjoyed having the freedom to talk openly.

"Before going to college, one of the things I really enjoyed was listening to records in my bedroom, in particular one song written and sung by Ricky Nelson, 'The Garden Party.' Then one day my dad walked by my bedroom and heard the part of the lyrics that said, 'You can't please everyone, so you've got to please yourself.' He strode into my room and gave me a lecture on how you have to please others before yourself. From that day on, my father forbid me to listen to that song while I lived in his house.

"If you knew my father, you would understand why this song wasn't a big hit with him. My father was brought up in Pennsylvania. He was a lawyer and a very giving man who believed in finding time to help others no matter how busy you were. He served on the board of Legal Aid, the Airport Authority, and the School Board. He even found time to volunteer at our church. So you can see why he found those lyrics disturbing.

"The day I left for college, my dad divorced my mother. I guess he had stayed to please everyone but himself. The divorce was extremely difficult for me. I promised myself that if I got married, it would be forever. That was probably because I had a good idea who I was going to marry—Larry, my best friend of fourteen years.

"Larry and I laughed, played, and shared everything. We were inseparable. We dated throughout high school and shortly after exchanged wedding vows. My husband's career moved us from Pennsylvania to Florida. Larry owned and operated a travel agency. The business entailed a lot of traveling and staying away from home for days at a time.

"Before I knew it, we were married eleven years. The time passed so fast. I think time seemed to pass so quickly for me because while Larry was away I kept busy tending after our very active little boy, attending law school, and keeping things on the home front in order.

"I always really looked forward to our vacation time, when the three of us would be together for a week or two. Usually we spent our vacation visiting our family and friends in Pennsylvania.

"One year my sister and her husband surprised us and arranged for us to stay overnight at a bed and breakfast while they watched our then four-year-old son. What a treat! Finally, we would have a little time together, just the two of us.

"As we drove to the hotel, my husband seemed annoyed and agitated instead of happy to be getting away together. We called it an early night. The next morning we went to breakfast. My husband sat very quietly, as if in deep thought. I was wide awake and drinking coffee when my husband looked me straight in the eyes and announced, 'I'm gay!'

"An internal voice echoed loudly, 'Gay? Did he say gay?' It felt like an instant out-of-body experience, as though I had left my body and was watching someone else. I was totally devastated. I didn't know what to do. I felt numb from the neck down. No, make that from the tip of my head to my toes.

"Larry, now relieved to be out of the closet, wanted to explain every little detail of the double life he had been leading. I wasn't ready for all that. The words, 'I'm gay,' hadn't even begun to penetrate into my brain yet. How could I possibly handle processing any more information? I kept hearing sounds come from his mouth, but I heard only my inner voice as it said, 'I can't believe I had no clue whatsoever.' Eleven years with my best friend, husband, and the father of my son were about to be destroyed.

"That day we had plans to visit and stay with a friend of my husband's. Larry drove to his friend's house, and when we arrived, still not over the devastation of Larry's news, I tried to act normally—or as normally as I could. I didn't dare tell a soul what my husband had revealed to me. I guess that part of my Italian upbringing kicked in.

"All day my mind played the same words over and over: 'He's gay,' followed by, 'What am I going to do?'

"We ended our vacation earlier than we had originally planned and returned home. For two weeks I didn't know what to think or do. I just went through the motions of everyday life, wondering how we could make this work. A divorce seemed to be the only choice, but at the time we had no money for a divorce.

"Larry suggested we stay together and live our separate lives until I finished law school. Boy, did I have a lot of thinking to do. I had only a year and a half left to complete law school, and I wasn't about to quit. I also knew that financially I wasn't ready to be thrust into single parenthood. So I agreed to live with Larry until I graduated.

"It was very difficult to live with my husband knowing he had a double life. Sometimes a day felt as long as a year. There were days I felt the situation would never end. . . .days when the only thing that got me through was the thought that staying together and finishing law school would guarantee a future for my son and me.

"I depended on the counseling I received from my therapist. Eventually I was able to talk about the whole situation, but at first only to Peggy and

Sara, my old college friends, mainly because I knew how open and nonjudgmental they were. As for family and friends, Larry and I agreed they only needed to know that our marriage just wasn't working. Our friends had a hard time believing this, though, because they knew we never fought and were truly each other's best friend.

"I finished law school and decided it was time to start a new life for my son and me. I interviewed at and was hired by a law firm in another state. This began a rewarding career in family law in a place we happily call home."

When Larry told Audrey he was gay, he wasn't the only one who came out of the closet that day. Behind Larry came two horses—a thoroughbred and a dead horse. The dead horse said to Audrey, "Your life is ruined. Don't tell anyone. Just run, get divorced, drop out of school!" The thoroughbred was Larry's mindset that said, "What if?" "Why not?" and "Let's try."

"What if we live separate lives together? Why not finish law school? Let's try it."

Audrey had two options. She could drag the dead horse out of the closet, seek no support, end the marriage hastily, and guarantee the self-fulfilling prophecy that her life was ruined. Or she could put on her lawyer's hat and think analytically, weigh all the facts, and use problem-solving skills. In other words, avoid getting on the dead horse altogether.

Audrey did just that when she opted to ride the second horse out of the closet. Although not an easy task, Audrey saddled up for a change she had never planned on. For a year and a half, one day at a time, Audrey rode a thorough-bred down a bumpy trail that led to a happy, new, stable life.

Today Larry and Audrey are still friends. Audrey remarried. I have a feeling it will be forever this time.

Oh, one more thing. Remember the song that Audrey's dad didn't like? He would be so proud to know that Audrey always finds time to please others—as well as herself. She is president of the local bar association and serves on numerous boards in her community, including Legal Aid which, by the way, provides legal assistance to women who can't afford representation in divorce proceedings.

CHAPTER TWELVE

The Talking Horse

Did you know that the one thing people fear most is public speaking? Most people say that they would rather jump out of a plane first—with a parachute, of course—than speak in front of a group of people.

Now that's not true in my case. I love to talk to groups—the bigger the group the better. Believe it or not, it actually energizes me.

In grade school I recall overhearing one teacher tell another that I must have been born talking. I will never forget how sore my wrists were from staying after school and writing on the blackboard at least a zillion times, "I will not talk in class." At least once a week I could always count on Mrs. Ellie, whom I secretly named the Dragon Lady, to send me to the principal's office for talking in class. I didn't mind, though. The principal was a truly nice man, and we would have the best talks together. Go figure. Back then I got punished for talking; today I get paid big bucks for doing the same thing!

I have never understood why people have a fear of public speaking. I must admit, however, that last year when a school superintendent hired me to motivate an academic team, I did have visions of a very old retired teacher named Mrs. Ellie hobbling to the front of the room, grabbing me, and yelling, "Young lady, come with me! You haven't learned a thing. You're still talking!"

Luckily for me this was just a fleeting thought, and the fear lasted for only a few seconds. But while the thought of Mrs. Ellie is fresh in my mind, I want to tell you about another woman whose first name is Ellen.

Ellen is a friend who talks as much as I do, but she wasn't born talking like I was. As a matter of fact, Ellen was born with a cleft palate and a harelip. The doctors surmised Ellen's birth defects were probably caused by antibiotics that were prescribed to her mother to fight pneumonia in her first trimester of pregnancy.

Ellen's mother was a nurse, and her dad was a plumber. They were also the proud parents of two other children who were several years older than Ellen. As you can imagine, with three children to raise and the usual bills, there was little income to spare at the end of the month, but somehow her parents managed to save enough money for three operations, all of which were performed while Ellen was an infant. Ellen's parents had hoped that the surgeries would make her speech clearer and her defects less obvious to others.

Unfortunately, according to Ellen, this was not the case. "I sat alone on the school bus. Let's put it this way: I wasn't exactly part of the 'in' group. Sometimes kids could be cruel. Making new friends was hard for me because I didn't trust people. To make matters worse, I was singled out by my teachers as being different from the other kids every time they would announce, 'Ellen, it's time for your speech class.'

"I hated speech class. Even there I was different. Some kids stuttered, some slurred their words or had a lisp. But they all improved, while I struggled just to sound normal. I would have given anything to trade places with any one of them.

"My parents encouraged me to keep going to speech class, hoping it would take the social stigma away from me. I wished everyone could be just like my brother and sister. I could always count on them to make me feel normal. To them, I was just little Ellie.

"By the time I went to Catholic high school, I had become very quiet and withdrawn. I didn't join any school clubs, although, looking back, I probably could have been the champion of the debate team. Since I had so few friends, all I did was study. What else was there to do? I was one smart kid and always made the National Honor Society.

"Even if I had wanted to go to college, there was little money for that. But when it came time to graduate from high school, I knew just what I wanted to do. I wanted to become a certified public accountant. My guidance counselor, however, had other plans for my life. She made it clear to me that girls didn't become CPAs, and she recommended that I become a bookkeeper.

"I didn't want to be a bookkeeper. Once more I was not being treated as normal. I could read between the lines. I was being told to 'work in the background' and not up front because I was different.

"Somehow I ended up becoming a medical technician, staying in the background of the doctors. The work was okay; I just didn't have a passion for it. I saw it as just another thing my guidance counselor had thought I should do.

"I became very independent and wasn't influenced easily by anyone until I met Bruce. He was a top mechanic for the county even though he was legally blind. Bruce was incredibly smart and could see life so clearly, despite his blindness. Nothing, I mean nothing, could stop him from doing what he wanted.

"When Bruce was two, a doctor discovered that the retina in one of his eyes was completely detached and the other was partially detached. There was no cure or any way to correct his lack of vision. But through the years he never gave up hope that, one day, eye transplants would become available.

"Bruce became the love of my life and my personal motivator. He believed in me so much that he encouraged me to go back to school to fulfill my dreams of becoming a CPA. And he did this at a time in his life when most people would have chosen to bury their head under the covers and never come out.

"At just thirty-two years old, Bruce was asked to see things differently, through his employer's eyes, because of an accident in the county garage. One freezing cold day in New Jersey, a truck full of pesticide chemicals entered the county garage late in the day for repairs. It came in so late that the work was scheduled to be done the next day. When Bruce and the other mechanics returned in the morning, they were exposed to deadly chemicals that had leaked from the truck overnight.

"At the hospital, all were given a successful antidote—all, that is, except for Bruce. The doctors knew that the cure would interfere with what little vision Bruce had left. The poison that stayed in his system made him nauseous and lethargic for months. Whenever Bruce showered, his body would reek of a chemical odor that seemed to seep out of every pore in his skin.

"The doctors could not do anything to help Bruce that wouldn't result in total blindness. A supervisor strongly suggested that Bruce should look into retirement. He was now a risk to their insurance.

"At thirty-two he didn't want to retire. He loved his job, and he was the best darned mechanic the county had. We had two children, and now we were both out of work. We decided to pack up and move to Florida. For weeks on end Bruce tried getting a job without any luck. That's when he said, 'I have the perfect job! You always wanted to be a CPA. You go back to school, and I will take care of the house and our children.'

"It was a complete role reversal. I did my homework with my kids at night, and in the daytime I worked in a bank. I earned my associate's degree and my bachelor's degree and became an accountant.

"After graduating from college, I left the bank and went to work for a CPA for several months. I hated every minute of it. I was stuck in a back room all day where I processed tax returns for the wealthy. I had no contact with any people whatsoever.

"Then one day my boss wanted me to audit the books for a country club. I could tell he was very leery of sending me where someone might see me and hear my speech impairments. The client was extremely pleased with my work, and my boss was surprised at the bond the client and I had made. He recognized my qualities, but it was too late. I was burned out on his management style.

"That night after dinner I mentioned to Bruce that I wanted to quit and start my own consulting business.

"'Great!' Bruce said. 'Go get business cards made up.' He was always there, motivating me to reach for my dreams.

"My business cards looked terrific. The first and only card I ever used was the one I gave to the director of Meals on Wheels. I was hired as a consultant to straighten out their bookkeeping system, accounting for mostly grant and donor funds. I worked on this one account for sixty hours a week while Bruce cooked, cleaned, spoiled our children, and never once complained about my absence from home.

"After eight months I completed the project. It was time to say goodbye, not only to the director, but to a place I had learned to love—a place where people had big hearts and cared about those who needed help in the community. A place I would truly miss.

"I was both surprised and delighted when the director told me that she wanted me to stay on as a full-time employee. It was about ten A.M. when I accepted the job offer. At exactly eleven-thirty she gave me my first assignment. She said she had a speaking engagement that she could not attend and that I was to fill in for her.

"I answered, 'Me? You want me to speak for you? No, I don't think so!' I couldn't believe she would ask such a thing of me, considering my speech problem.

"She asked, 'Why not?'

"Stunned, I answered, 'Because of the way I talk.'

"'Ellie, you just speak differently,' she said. 'Sometimes you talk too fast. Just take your time and slow down. This is only a group that wants to know about our fundraising. Who knows more than you about the subject?'

"At twelve noon I stood in front of a room filled with a hundred and fifty people. As they quietly waited for me to begin talking, I stared at the door at the back of the room. Only one thing kept me from running out the door—the thought of how proud Bruce would be to know that I was right in front of the room and not in the back. In the front, where I had longed to be my whole life.

"As I started to speak, I could hear my boss's words echo softly in the back of my mind: 'Take your time and slow down.' I enjoyed talking to the group that day about a topic I had a passion for—Meals on Wheels.

"It's been fourteen years since I addressed that group. Today, almost daily, I am still speaking to groups about Meals on Wheels. Come to think of it, not much has changed in all those years. I still love my job, my husband is still the love of my life, and I'm still in awe of a woman who believed in me so much that she promoted me to director of Meals on Wheels the day she retired."

Isn't it amazing how Bruce, who was legally blind, blazed the trail for Ellie's dreams? It's as if Bruce had a thoroughbred all saddled up and patiently waiting for Ellie to dismount her dead horse named Handicap.

Handicap was not really Ellie's dead horse, but rather one a teacher had given her to take care of many years earlier. Ellie was a good student who always did what her teachers asked her to do, so she never left that horse alone once. That is, until a woman came along and gave Ellie a shove that knocked her off the dead horse that had held her back for years.

It's no wonder she had never spoken to a group of people before. That dead horse must have weighed well over a thousand pounds! How could anyone manage to drag it to the front of a room? Sure, when Ellie's boss knocked her off the dead horse, she suffered a few scrapes and bruises—but not enough to stop her from mounting the thoroughbred Bruce had so lovingly boarded—a lively horse named Courage!

Recognizing that you're sitting on a dead horse is sometimes the hardest thing to do. If you're lucky, like Ellie, you just might meet someone who cares about you enough to give you the nudge you need to dismount your dead horse—even a horse that rightfully is not yours.

Today I am on the board of directors for Meals on Wheels, and I regularly have the opportunity to listen to Ellie speak, as do so many people. Ellie made up for not being in any clubs back in school by joining the boards of the Florida Council on Aging, the Florida Association of Senior Service Providers, and the Florida Restaurant Association. She's president of the Florida Association of Senior Nutrition Providers, and helps many more.

Ellie, we are really listening to you and love all that you do for the community!

CHAPTER THIRTEEN

A Sorry Excuse For a Horse

My next two chapters are about two remarkable women, both named Sharon. The first is about my friend Sharon Straw. Sharon is one of those people who literally lights up a room when she walks into it, and then she sells you the house that the room is in. At least, that's what happened to me on more that one occasion.

My first introduction to Sharon was on a long-distance phone call I made from Ohio to a Florida real estate office. Sharon just happened to pick up the phone that day. I met Sharon in person soon afterwards, when she picked up my husband and me at the airport in hope of selling us a house. Within the first five minutes of meeting her, it was evident to both of us that a wonderful friendship had begun.

Six years have passed since the day I befriended Sharon, and so have hundreds of cups of coffee we've sipped over laughs and chats. We've chatted about everything we hold dear—about relationships, our goals, a son she adores and, of course, this book—the book I dreamed of writing about women getting off of their dead horses, which, by the way, Sharon had me believing was a best-seller before I even started to put a pen to paper, or should I say, fingers to laptop!

Sharon has a way of making you feel like a winner before you even know there is a contest to enter. If I could give one gift to every woman, other than my book, of course, it would be just ten minutes with Sharon—after which I would set them free on the world. Then you would see progress, real progress in action.

Obviously I can't do that, but not just because the logistics would be impossible. Another reason is that lately Sharon is so busy selling real estate that I can't even get ten minutes of her time. What I do get is her voice mail, but I really don't mind because it's always so uplifting. She actually takes the time to change her voice mail message every single day. Most of her messages are the usual stuff. You know, "I'm not available but leave a message at the tone. I'll call you back."

More unusual are Sharon's closing questions, which I actually write on my desk calendar while I wait for the beep. Here are just a few of my favorites:

* What's something you're excited about today?

* If you knew you couldn't fail, what would you go after?

* What's something you're going to accomplish today?

* What's special about your life today?

After what seemed to be an eternity, Sharon and I finally connected for lunch. One of the first things I asked her was where she gets all those thought-provoking questions at the end of her voice mail.

Sharon told me she gets up every morning and asks herself a new positive question and enjoys sharing the question with her friends and clients on her voice mail.

"And you do this because—?" I asked, puzzled.

I didn't get an answer for a few seconds. Sharon seemed to be preoccupied as she gazed into the distance.

Then she said, "I do this because I want people to know how I think. That's important to me.

"When I was a child, I never let people know what I was thinking. That is, except for my mother, who knew just what I was thinking! I would write a card to her almost every day expressing what was on my mind.

"I started writing her cards at the age of five. In every card I wrote to my mother, one thing stayed the same: The line that said, 'I'm sorry.' Sorry for not doing my homework, sorry for not doing the dishes right, sorry for upsetting her, sorry for—well, you name it. Whatever it was, I was apologizing for it.

"It took some time, but I finally realized that no matter how many cards I wrote or how many times I would say 'I'm sorry,' I would never please my mother."

Sharon had no idea that her mother's unreachable standards were actually a preview of the challenges that would lie ahead.

One day in her late twenties, she finally stood up for herself by not saying, "I'm sorry."

"I was married at the time and had decided to quit my secretarial job to raise my son. When he was about five, I decided it was time to go back into the workforce. Every Sunday I would glance at the classified section in our local paper. I never looked for a specific job because I knew I could do anything if given the chance.

"One job caught my eye. It read Coordinator for Charter Yachts. I had no idea what that meant, but yachts sounded good, so I applied and was hired on the spot.

"For two weeks I worked part-time, and two weeks later I was assigned to a full-time position. Just two weeks after that, I was promoted to the position of Director of Charter Yachts.

"I loved my job. I enjoyed working with the customers, although most of my work was accomplished by phone. When I wasn't on the phone, I would listen to the salesmen give their sales pitch to potential customers.

"At the time all of the salesmen were men. After hearing the old, worn-out sales pitch several times, I knew I could sell yachts better than them. I approached the owner of the company and asked if I could have a shot at selling yachts. He smirked and said, 'Okay, but you will be asking for your old job back sooner than you think.'

"One year later I was outselling every other salesman. I even sold yachts on the phone. Mind you, I had never been on a boat and didn't know the difference between the bow and the stern of a ship. I believed knowledge was a powerful thing, but you didn't need to know everything about everything to sell. You just needed to like people and be honest. If a customer asked a question and I didn't know the answer, I would simply tell my customer, 'I don't know, but I will definitely find out for you.'

"As my sales increased my pay seemed to plateau, and little Post-It notes started appearing attached to my pay. The notes read, 'You are making more than the men!' I felt as though I should apologize, but I could not figure out for what.

"I worked hard and sold more forty-foot yachts than anyone. And you won't believe what happened next. We started selling sixty-foot yachts. I sold the first three in four months. I was so excited, I couldn't wait to get my commission check.

"Friday came and so did my check, but I was stunned to discover that I made less selling the sixty-foot yachts than the forty-foot yachts. How could that be?

"I started asking the all-male sales team about the commission structure, only to find out that I was making less than each and every one of them— way less.

"I decided that it was time for my boss to know just what I was thinking. I decided to confront him. It was a very difficult thing for me to do back then. Nevertheless, I stood up for myself. I wasn't that little girl anymore who so easily said 'I'm sorry.' I was a woman, and I wasn't sorry for making more sales than the men. Maybe it was time for the other sales-men to listen in on my sales approach.

"The owner, who was my boss, made it perfectly clear that he wasn't going to change my commission because I was a woman. Once again I did feel sorry—sorry for him. I quit and sued.

"The court awarded me the commission back pay, but I never actually received the money because the owner of the company went bankrupt. I often wondered whether, if he had hired more women, he would have had such a sorry-looking bottom line."

At a tender age, Sharon's hypercritical mother helped her climb onto a pony that grew up to be a sorry excuse for a horse—a dead horse that she came to recognize in her twenties as a mindset she had programmed to apologize for everything.

Sharon dismounted that Sorry horse the day she went face to face with her boss. She then mounted a thoroughbred named Glad—glad she had left her dead horse behind.

It's funny now that I think of it; "glad" was the first thing Sharon said when we first met. Her exact words were, "Glad to meet you, I'm Sharon Straw." Sharon, you have no idea how glad I was to meet you. Just between you and me, though, aren't you just a little bit sorry for all that phone tag we play? Sorry I asked.

CHAPTER FOURTEEN

Horse Shoes

Can you imagine a woman in America who doesn't like shoes? For that matter, how about a woman who doesn't have more than one pair of shoes in her closet?

Although the woman you're about to be introduced to had a closet full of shoes, she had no idea that she would wear out all of them as she traveled on a mental and physical journey to meet a child who had just one pair of shoes that she actually didn't own.

Kind, unselfish, and loving are the only words in the English language I can think of to describe this second Sharon, a woman whose shoes it would be hard to fill.

Sharon's dream was to have a child even though she was a forty-year-old single woman who worked paycheck-to-paycheck in New York City.

I believe it wasn't the sound of her biological clock ticking that kept Sharon awake at night. I believe it was the faint sound of a young mother's faraway footsteps as she left a building empty-handed. . . .a mother who loved her child so much that she entrusted the infant to a place where she hoped and prayed her child would have a chance at a better life. I believe the faint sound of this mother's footsteps carried her hopes into Sharon's heart.

"I didn't want my life to pass by, only to remember in my golden years that I forgot to have kids," Sharon said as she gazed at me earnestly. "I wanted to be a mother so I could love a child the way my mother had loved me. I couldn't think of a greater gift to give a child.

"I thought hard and long about what I was about to do—artificial insemination. I had no fear about being a single parent. My desire to be a mother overrode all the fear. Sure, I knew that financially it meant that I wouldn't be living in a mansion or driving a BMW. If a partner came into my life down the road, he would get a package deal. I knew that a lot of responsibility accompanied my choice. But it was just that—my choice.

"I contacted a sperm bank and began a process as bizarre as any novel. I was sent catalogs of profiles, including resumes, photos, family history, education, goals, and the aspirations of the donors. Most were young college students looking to make money. It was like shopping in a catalog for just the right outfit, and I found it! That was the easy part.

"Next were the injections I gave myself every day to manipulate my cycle, the whole time knowing, as the doctor had informed me, that there was only a slim chance the artificial insemination would work the first time.

"The doctor was right; it didn't work. But I had a backup plan already in progress. While I was attempting artificial insemination, I also contacted an adoption agency. I found it comforting to know that I had other options. What I didn't know was what a challenge it was for a single white American female to adopt a white American child. Next to impossible. No, make that impossible!

"Understandably, a mother who is giving up her child wants a family unit of two parents to adopt the child. So, for a single woman trying to adopt a child in America, the red tape is endless. But I wasn't giving up.

"I read everything about adoptions I could get my hands on. I spent countless hours on the Internet and in the book stores. Finally, I decided to adopt in a country that would bestow upon me my dream of motherhood: Russia.

"The U.S. adoption agency gave me grueling amounts of paperwork that stacked a mile high—no exaggeration! Every page I carefully filled out had to be notarized and hand delivered with a state seal that cost twenty-five dollars per document. I was told that the process could take well over a year.

"As I waited, more tasks were asked of me. I needed to provide bank statements, reference letters, proof of insurance, medical records, and a home study that included blueprints and photos of my home.

"The most awkward task was a home visit from a state agency. I remember that day all too well. The doorbell rang, and as I opened the door I didn't see a thing until I looked down. There stood a woman about four feet, eleven inches tall. Being five-foot-eleven myself, I bent over to greet her and welcomed her into my house. She was from the state agency to which I was about to pay a thousand dollars so this woman could put my life under a microscope and then place it in—what else?—a red tape file. We spent four long hours together, during which I answered personal questions I never imagined I would be asked.

"My emotions were on a roller coaster. I worked every day, and what little time I had left I spent learning about adopting a Russian child from an orphanage or, as the Russian system refers to them, 'baby homes.' Months passed by, and the only thing that seemed to happen was more paperwork to fill out every day.

"As I was researching Russian adoptions on the Internet, I came across several alarming sites about couples who unknowingly adopted children who suffered from mental development disorders, amongst many other serious health problems. These were illnesses that simply could not be recognized by a layperson.

"One article listed two world-renowned developmental psychologists who were experts in identifying potential health problems in the adoption of foreign children.

"I contacted one of the doctors, who was located in New York, my own back yard. He explained that the American adoption agency could request photos, records, and a short videotape of the child I was interested in adopting. For a two-hundred-fifty-dollar fee, he would review the information and give me a report of his findings.

"That was money well spent. In four months I had selected three children, and I fell in love with each one. The doctor reviewed information on each child, all of whom he diagnosed with potentially serious problems, ranging from brain damage to socialization problems.

"It would have been impossible for me, as a single working parent, to take on any medical hardship. I could tell the doctor was broken-hearted when he phoned me with the news of the third child. I assured him that his skills were a gift to me; that I was making a life-changing decision, and that I didn't want him to compromise his standards.

"Over the next several months the doctor and I became friends. I respected his opinion and the opinion of his wife, who was a neonatal physician.

"Early one morning I FedExed one more package to the doctor, concerning a child who took my breath away every time I looked at her photo. Her name was Anastasya, which translated in English to 'anesthesia.' Why anyone would name a child that was beyond me. She was the most beautiful child I had ever seen.

"At midnight that night my phone rang. I reached across the bed to pick up the receiver and answered drowsily, only to hear, 'She is beautiful. Go get her!'

"This was only the beginning of—what else?—more red tape from the American and Russian governments. First, my papers were processed, and I was approved to go to Russia—not as easy as it sounds. It's not as if you can book a flight for tomorrow and just go. You have to get a visa, which takes time.

"Finally, all my traveling papers were in order, as were those of my sister, who accompanied me on the eleven-hour-long flight to Russia. My sister was a camera buff who I knew would capture every second of this mother-and-daughter union.

"Our airline tickets were the least of my expenses. I had to hire a translator, a driver, and a host family to live with, and there were plenty of Russian court fees, not to mention all the gifts that the American adoption agency had coached me to take to everyone in Russia—and I do mean everyone—who was involved in the adoption process.

"When we landed in Russia, it was nightfall. Our interpreter and driver were waiting for us. After the introductions we were whisked off to the home of our host family, where we would stay for the next few days.

"The following morning, while waiting for our driver to take me to see

Anastasya, I noticed the townspeople walking by. All had scowls on their faces; not one smiled. They wore old clothes in shades of dingy brown and gray. I felt as though I was back in 1929, in the middle of a movie about the Great Depression. I began to think about the similarities between the townspeople and the weather. The sky was dark gray; the air was damp and cold; it chilled you to your bones.

"My thoughts were interrupted by my driver pulling alongside the curb. I knew what lay ahead would be wonderful. My sister helped me load a big bag filled with the gifts that were expected of me into the car, together with her camera gear. The interpreter, my sister, and I all squeezed in, and off we went.

"During the twenty-minute drive, I must have asked a hundred times, 'Are we there yet?' I was feeling excited, nervous, and anxious, all at once. Finally, my sister said, 'It's around this bend.'

"We turned the corner, and there stood a huge, gray, cold, bleak, dreary, heart-wrenching stone building surrounded by a tall black iron fence. As I got out of the car and walked toward the rusty old gate, I felt as if I were walking into a prison.

"The iron gate was heavy, but I gave it a push, and it opened with a squeak. The entrance doors were extremely massive and heavy to open. Once inside, I noticed a musty mildew smell that must have come from the tufted wet leather on the inside of the door, used in a vain attempt to keep the cold out.

"We were directed to go up a flight of ten stairs into a waiting room. I'll never forget the wall going up the stairs. It was the only one with color. Half of the wall was painted yellow.

"At the top of the stairs we were greeted by the director of the so-called 'Baby House Number Five'—still an orphanage to me. She was a hefty Russian woman with a deep voice who showed us into a room that was empty with the exception of one small picnic table and a few school chairs.

"I was definitely nervous. I didn't understand one word of what was being said as my interpreter talked to the director in Russian. The woman was still talking as she was leaving the room.

"Within seconds the woman came back with Anastasya—a vision I will never forget. There she stood in an old red tattered dress at least two sizes too big for her frail little body. Her hair was in the funniest looking pigtails I had ever seen. One pigtail was sticking straight up, the other straight out of the side of her head. Her shoes are the very things that make me cry till this day, totally worn out with hardly any color left, except the number three written in black marker on top of each shoe. Anastasya was simply known as Number Three.

"This year-and-a-half-old angelic child was so well adjusted. Later I was told that she had actually mothered the other seventeen toddlers in the home. She was a blessing to more than just me.

"The entire time I spent with Anastasya my sister took photos, but only one says it all—the close-up of those shoes bearing the number three on each toe.

"Anastasya reached out to me with her tiny hand, and she took me to a room filled wall-to-wall with cribs to show me where she slept. It was impossible to walk between the cribs, they were so close to each other. Although the room was clean, the battered cribs and the condition of the once-white walls were a disheartening sight.

"Anastasya led the way to a room filled with toddlers—seventeen toddlers, to be exact. All sat perfectly still with one exception—the movement of their tiny hands. Hands that slowly and deliberately maneuvered spoons much bigger than their little mouths into a hot bowl of soup. The bowls sat on top of a bib each child had tied to their neck, only inches away from their tiny chins.

"I was stunned to see these toddlers feeding themselves. I couldn't understand how so much was expected of such a small child. When I asked if any of them ever spilled hot soup on themselves, I was told that they just didn't. If they did they would not eat.

"At seventeen months and younger, these children drank out of adult cups with no assistance. Unlike in America, the potty training simply meant that each toddler had a pot—an actual cooking pot—that they would retrieve under a counter, which they would use, clean, and put back.

"I couldn't wait to take Anastasya home so I could spoil her with the love and affection she had never experienced. That day I was allowed just enough time to take Anastasya to get a photo for her passport. Then I had to take her back to that heart-wrenching place. It was, without a doubt, the hardest thing I ever had to do. She was mine and I was hers, but we had to wait three weeks for the red tape to go through in the Russian courts.

"Most adopting parents stay the three weeks in Russia, but I had a job back home and I was single, so off I went back to New York for what was the longest three weeks of my entire life.

"My mother accompanied me back to Russia. I hoped only for one thing—that Anastasya would love me the way I loved my mother. Once again, in Russia I couldn't help but notice that I was surrounded by gray skies, gray buildings, and gray-looking people. This time it didn't faze me, though, because I had a rainbow brighter than the NBC peacock in my heart to share with Anastasya.

"As was asked of me, I brought clothes for Anastasya to the orphanage, including a coat and a pair of new shoes. One might say I have a 'thing' for shoes. And I have every hope that my daughter will carry on the tradition! The old dress she wore, along with her shoes, would be given to another child who would now be known only as Number Three.

"I could tell my mother was experiencing the same emotions I had the first time I entered this dreary-looking institution; however, her facial expression changed the moment Anastasya entered the room. Anastasya went right to her new grandmother. Every time I tried to hold her she would have a fit. I couldn't understand what was wrong. My daughter didn't like me!

"That was until my mother made the observation that the only women Anastasya knew were her caretakers, older, big-busted, robust Russian women like my mother. My mother's observation made me—a five-foot-eleven small-busted slender woman—feel much better.

"After a short visit with Anastasya, she was taken, along with the clothes I brought her, into another room where she was stripped of her clothing, including those God-awful shoes that identified her as Number Three.

"For the first time I dressed my daughter from head to toe. For the first time Anastasya was about to step out into the world beyond the doors and the grounds she had never left since the day she arrived.

"With my mother by my side, I held Anastasya in my arms as she cried and screamed when my mother opened the oversized, musty-smelling castlelike doors. Together all of us took the first step out into a cold, blustery day. As snowflakes fell gently upon our faces, the doors closed and Anastasya stopped crying."

If you can't figure out what Sharon's dead horse was, there is a good reason. You see, Sharon never had a dead horse. However, Sharon was exposed to many dead horses every step of the way to her dream. They are society's dead horses, mindsets of those who have created red tape and boundaries for single women adopting children, and for all those wishing to adopt, both in the U.S.A. and in Russia.

Society did, does, and will always have dead horses. Woman can, will, and must always remember that they have the choice of mounting a thoroughbred—a mindset that always asks, "What if?" "Why not?" and "Let's try." This mindset can jump over any hurdle, including society's dead horses. Sharon did just that.

It's been four years since Anastasya's little feet, wearing new shoes, took her first steps on the soil of her new home, America. This happy, fun, energetic, curious, bright, and well-adjusted child has since worn out dozens of shoes. Every step she takes leaves lasting footprints in so many people's minds and hearts.

Something in my gut tells me two things. One, that Anastasya will always have lots of shoes in her closet—shoes that she will wear out as she walks hand-in-hand with her mother on a life journey filled with love. Two, that Sharon and Anastasya will always be in the winner's circle, proudly sitting in the saddle of a thoroughbred, with one exception, of course—dismounting for the briefest of moments to replace worn out horse shoes.

LADIES...DISMOUNT!

CHAPTER FIFTEEN

The Tale of Two Horses

When my future husband came to pick me up on our first date, he looked around my kitchen and asked, "What kind of dog do you have?"

"I don't have a dog," I answered.

He looked a little puzzled. "Then why do you have a dog bowl in your kitchen?"

"When I was a child, we had lots of dogs," I explained, "but for some reason we never had one for more than a few years. Of course, as a child I couldn't understand how anyone could give up a dog. I never understood my parents' reasons—like the landlord who didn't like dogs or the neighbor who was a chronic complainer about our dog barking—much less their situation. At times my parents barely got by raising four children, even though they both often worked two jobs. At the end of a long day, they hardly had any energy left to tend to us kids, let alone a dog.

"Eighteen years ago I promised myself that once I was on my own I would get a dog. I vowed I would love it as though it was my child, and I would never give it away. That's why I bought that dog bowl in the kitchen!"

I smiled expectantly at Mike, who still looked a little blank.

"And?" he prodded, raising his eyebrows.

"Well," I continued, "when the day came to spread my wings, I flew from Rhode Island to Pittsburgh for a wonderful job that entailed extensive travel in a territory of twelve states. Back then, as much as I wanted a dog, I knew it wouldn't be fair to get one just to put it in a kennel while I traveled. Besides, that would mean I would have to break my promise to myself that I would never give my dog away even for one day." I shrugged. "Somehow the traveling never stopped. As you can see, I'm still traveling eighteen years after leaving the nest."

Mike nodded as if my story made perfect sense. Then he grinned and said, "Are you ready to go?"

Four months after that first date, Mike and I married on a sunny, cool September afternoon. I never thought I would be happier than the day we became husband and wife... until the morning of November 27th, some two months later—my birthday. That morning Mike handed me a card as I was making a pot of coffee. Tears of joy spilled from my eyes as I read it. The card said,

"Happy birthday! I love you, and P.S.—I didn't know what kind of dog you wanted, so this card is good for one puppy anytime."

I held on to that card for a few years before I cashed it in. My traveling for work came to a halt the day I opened my own business. I did take one last trip that day with Mike, however. We drove about an hour from our house to an Air Force base where a young couple had sheltie puppies for sale.

With my birthday card in hand, we entered the couple's home, where we saw two adorable sheltie puppies. One was the runt of the litter and quite frisky. She ran by us, grabbed her mother's tail in her mouth, and held on for dear life as her mother raced toward the door, barking at a bird flying overhead.

As we watched the runt scampering and sliding behind her mother, I felt a gentle brush of soft puppy fur against my legs. When I looked down, my eyes met the gaze of the gentlest, most regal brown eyes I ever saw. According to the breeder, she was the calm puppy of the litter. Her mother had had seven pups, but only these two were left.

I knew the moment that I looked into those loving brown eyes that this was the dog I was going to choose—until the little runt popped her head under her sister's front legs as if to say, "Me! Pick me!"

What a difficult choice I had to make that day. I had waited eighteen years for this dog, and I could only pick one. Who would I leave behind—the runt who was quite active, but looked weaker than her sister? I felt as though she needed someone to protect her. Or the queenly brown-eyed, independent and self-sufficient one?

"Luckily," I thought, "I don't have to choose." I asked Mike to pick one.

But he just smiled and said, "No, you pick."

Before I tell you who we picked, I want to share a story with you about Janice and the day she was asked to "Pick one!"

Janice is a beautiful, slender, soft-spoken brunette in her early thirties. She exuded confidence and class in her every word as she unfolded a fascinating story—one she had held close to her heart for a very long time in hopes of protecting those she loved.

"I was eleven years old when I was asked to make the most difficult decision of my life," Janice began. "My father, who I loved and adored, called for me as he stood on the back porch. Our home was like something right out of a magazine. It sat in the middle of ten acres of lush countryside in the Midwest. This was a place any child would have loved to live.

"My father was the vice president of a major corporation. He provided our family with everything we could ever want, including twenty-two horses, guinea pigs, cats and dogs, and numerous other four-legged critters. My mother claimed every single one to be hers. How she loved her pets, especially her horses! My mother had developed a passion for horses during her challenging childhood. Whenever difficult times arose in her home, she found comfort in talking to her trusted horse, a companion who loved her unconditionally.

"I, on the other hand, would handle stressful times between my parents by simply disappearing. You could see me, but I wasn't there. Unlike my siblings, I was an extremely independent child with great self-esteem. As a child I truly believed that one day I would be extraordinary and unique.

"Although I knew my parents loved me, their love for each other seemed to unravel on a daily basis. My father was a kind, intelligent man who loved my mother enough to know she was falling out of love with being married. Being as understanding as he was, he honored her wish to separate.

"Today I think of how hard it must have been for him to call out my name from the back porch, knowing that he was going to ask me to make a decision that would change my life forever. After I ran up to stand next to my dad, he leaned over to meet my eyes and gently broke the news that he and Mom were splitting up, and that I had to make a choice between living with him or my mother.

"I loved my dad, my brothers and sisters, the farm, my teachers, and the town we lived in, but I felt my mom was weak and that someone had to look out for her; so I picked my mother. I guess you could say my mother was a free spirit at heart and perhaps a bit impulsive-particularly the day she piled a few personal belongings, along with a TV, dogs, cats, and guinea pigs—oh, yes, and me—into a wood-crate-sided old farm truck that looked like a prop from *The Beverly Hillbillies*. After packing the truck we drove off into the sunset without telling anyone, including my dad.

"We headed south. My mother had little if any money, no job, and no place to live, but she kept driving anyway. After almost a day of driving, we turned off the highway and entered a small southern town where my mother finally parked the truck in front of a small, rundown ranch house she told me belonged to a friend of hers. The friend turned out to be a single woman with three kids whom my mother hadn't talked to or seen for sixteen years.

"My mother's so-called friend kindly invited us in, and we stayed for more time than I think she expected. In fact, we moved in with her.

"I experienced serious culture shock, produced both by the town and our living conditions. I was considered an undesirable Yankee in this southern town, and to top it off my mother was what the townspeople called a divorcée.

"One day when I came home after school, my mother told me that we had to leave her friend's house. I guess the woman had grown tired of us. That was when I realized my mother was a survivor who took every opportunity offered to her to get what she needed, including our next home—an old, beat-up trailer house that a married man she knew bought for her. We drove that dilapidated house on wheels out into the country until my mother spotted a piece of land in the middle of nowhere, and we became squatters.

"Before long my mother was dating a man who put up a fence for us around the land our trailer home was on. I also remember another man my mother befriended who dug us a shallow well that we hooked up to our trailer for water. The water was cold, and it had an orange tint to it. Believe me, this was a far cry from the gracious house we had lived in back north.

"I became known in school as the poor kid, the Yankee who talked funny. I was a straight-A student, but an outcast nevertheless. But my self-esteem and desire to one day be unique and to do something extraordinary was fueled by my classmates' cruelty and that so-called trailer home we lived in.

"My mother's dating seemed to fill her social calendar most evenings. While she painted the town red, I stayed up late studying, often frightened at the thought of the lack of security in our trailer. The windows didn't lock. The door was shaky at best, and the trailer was anchored on a piece of land in the middle of nowhere.

"Eventually we got to know the woman who owned the land next to us. I think she had a soft spot in her heart for us, because she called the owner of the land we were squatting on and got him to agree to let us stay there.

"My mother sent for her seven horses, even though we were barely surviving ourselves. We had little or no food, but she always made sure that the horses were fed, even before us.

"At the time I was much too young to realize that my mom had mental challenges. I just knew that I had to protect her. Seven years of living in that trailer passed by as slow as molasses, but my desire to be unique and to do something extraordinary never passed. It didn't matter to me what the other kids said. I could disappear even though they could still see me.

My self-esteem was like a shield that blocked me from them.

"At fifteen I met Tom, who became my boyfriend. We dated until I was twenty-one. His parents were a godsend. They always fed me and treated me like one of their family. High school graduation was approaching, and I had to decide what I wanted to do. I had no doubt that I was going to college to become extraordinary, unique, and successful. But there were two problems. I had no clue whatsoever what I would major in, and I was haunted by the fact that planning for college meant that I would have to make the painful decision to leave my mother behind.

"One day while talking to Tom, I told him I wanted to pick something that would make my dad proud. Tom suggested dental school. 'That's it,' I thought. 'I'll become a dentist. My dad will be proud.'

"My ability to study hard and the fact I was an excellent student helped me pay my college tuition with grants, student loans, and part-time jobs. I couldn't afford to live on campus, but I found three other girls who were looking for one more roommate to help pay the rent on a flat. All of them took my rent money, and all of them made fun of me. I was a college student, but still poor-still from a trailer with squatting rights.

"I studied extremely hard and stayed in school full-time, even in the summer. I did anything not to go back to the trailer. Don't get me wrong, I loved my mother; but I had made a painful decision to move forward with my life. During my third year of college I applied to dental school, even though I hadn't graduated yet. The school made a once-in-a-lifetime exception and granted me admission with only three years of undergraduate school."

Janice completed dental school with honors and then went on to become even more extraordinary—a world-renowned specialist, one of the top doctors in a highly specialized field. Today she is unquestionably a unique and successful woman whose peers travel from all around the world to attend her seminars.

Something tells me that when Janice teaches her peers, two old four-legged friends are standing by her side, the childhood ponies she nurtured all those years. I can almost see them, a beautiful thoroughbred named Compassion on her right and a powerful plow house named Self-esteem on her left.

I can't imagine how tough it must have been for eleven-year-old Janice to have to decide which parent she wanted to live with. Picking her father would certainly have been the easy choice for most children, but easy meant nothing compared to Janice's perception that her mom was weak and needed someone to protect her.

I can imagine, though, knowing Janice, that while her mother was packing up that old "Beverly Hillbillies" farm truck, Janice was mentally packing up those two ponies. She had tended to her faithful thoroughbred named Self-esteem from the time she was a toddler. Self-esteem was the horse she planned to ride on a life path to a unique place called Success. Compassion was the second pony, the pony that appeared on the back porch like magic on the day she decided to live with her mother. How many children do you know who would have given up all the privileges of living in a big house on a farm in a town where all their friends lived?

Equally amazing to me is how Janice's pony Compassion helped her tolerate the mental anguish of being taunted by classmates, not to mention the stigma of being the poor kid who lived in a rundown trailer home. Compassion was a powerful horse that Janice had groomed daily for years in hopes of protecting her mother. Janice spent a lot of time riding Compassion when she lived with her mother, but always managed to find time for Self-esteem, her favorite pony, the one that could handle any trail life took her on.

One day, as a young adult, Janice realized that her horse Compassion was taking her in circles. As much as she wanted to protect her mother, she saw that her mother's lifestyle wasn't going to change no matter how much longer Janice lived with her. It was time to board Compassion in a comfortable stable, saddle up Self-esteem, and find a new riding trail. She soon found a new trail to college, where she rode Self-esteem every day and visited Compassion in her spare time.

Janice was a remarkable child who never grabbed the reins of a dead horse named Poor Me, even when it looked her straight in the eyes and begged her to mount it. I chose to end this book with Janice's "tale of two horses," because I found her to be the only person I know who rode and nurtured two thoroughbreds as a child. She never had a dead horse at all.

From Janice, we can learn that it is possible not to get stuck on a dead horse and to ride two thoroughbreds at once. We just need to remember that sometimes we have to slow down and give our attention to one thoroughbred at a time.

As for the sheltie puppies, we took both of them home that day. We were lucky that we didn't have to choose between the two—the frisky little one who needed us, and the serene, self-sufficient one.

Janice didn't have that choice. She could have easily dragged around a dead horse named Poor Me her whole life. But she chose not to, and so can you. I think you would agree that Janice was always unique and extraordinary, a resilient, visionary child whose ponies grew up to be thoroughbreds while she matured to be a beautiful, successful, and compassionate woman.

Hey, Dad, I'll bet you're smiling at your extraordinary daughter who did pick you. . .for the rest of your life to be proud of her.

Breeds of Dead Horses

As we have seen, there are as many breeds of dead horses as there are women willing to ride them. Here is a list of some of the most common types of dead horses and the thoroughbreds that can replace them. Go ahead, ladies—dismount! Drop off those dead horses at the glue factory and gallop into the O.K. Corral!

GLUE FACTORY	O.K. CORRAL
I Can't	I Can
Blaming Others	Taking Responsibility
Settling for Less	Possibility
Self-Pity	Will
Childhood Programming	Grown-up Choice
Procrastination	Now
Pride	Receptive to Help
Despair	Hope
Guilt	Self-worth
Fear	Freedom
Handicap	Courage
Sorry	Glad
Delay	Perseverance
Whoa!	(Avoid that Dead Horse!)

Five Stages of Dead Horse Syndrome

Are you trying to ride a dead horse? Here is a handy way to tell if you are stuck on a dead horse. First, consider any areas of your life with which you are unhappy, frustrated, or dissatisfied. Then ask yourself which of these five categories most closely describes your present mindset.

Stage 1: DENIAL

You're in denial that you're on a dead horse if you're unhappy, but you say, "Why change? I'm doing just fine."

Stage 2: PASSIVE

You know you are on a dead horse, but hope no one notices. You are too fearful, hopeless, or insecure to change.

Stage 3: ACTIVE

You keep kicking the dead horse, hoping it'll get up and ride again.

Stage 4: REACTIVE

You fall off your dead horse, but get right back in the saddle again because it is comfortable; you're used to it.

Stage 5: PROACTIVE

You jump off your dead horse, mount a thoroughbred, and blaze a new trail!

Aunt Julia's Quiz

Okay, ladies - you've made it this far. Do you think you've got it? Take Aunt Julia's quiz to find out.

Q: What Is a Dead Horse?

A) A negative person

B) An ex-boyfriend or husband

C) A job you hate

D) A mindset you have programmed to resist change at all costs

A: The answer is D, and only D. If you are wondering whether you might be on a dead horse, just listen to that little voice inside your head. You know, the one that whispers, "I can't." "Why change now?" "It's their fault, not mine." "I'm too fat/short/stupid." "If only I/he/she did/had this or that." If you're still not sure, ask a friend. Your true friends are the first to notice your horse has died, but may be the last to tell you in fear of being stampeded by your dead horses!

Q: If Your Horse Is Dead, What Should You Do?

A) Drag it

B) Hope no one notices

C) It's B-B-Q time

D) Dismount

A: The correct answer is, of course, D. It's not always as easy to dismount as it sounds. Some of us may take a great deal of time to dismount, as did

Mary Ann, who sat on her dead horse for fourteen years complaining about her ex-husband. And how about Angie, the angelic old woman who waited until age eighty-two to climb off her dead horse? These women didn't have this book to read, but you do! So stop procrastinating. It's never too late! Dismount! Jump off and stay off, and whatever you do, don't look back.

Q: What Exactly Is A Thoroughbred?

A) An expensive horse

B) Men's cologne

C) A horse with an English accent

D) A new mindset

A: No doubt you picked D. A thoroughbred is a new mindset that asks "What if?" "Why not?" and "Let's try!"—a new mindset that will always blaze new trails, jump hurdles, and stay focused on your goal. Remember, you can't even get out of the starting gate when you enter a race on a dead horse. You need a thoroughbred to carry you to the winner's circle!

Q: If Your Feet Are Firmly On the Ground:

A) You can't walk

B) Your feet are dirty

C) Your toenails are too long

D) You can't take a risk

A: You got it right! The answer is D. So go ahead, take a risk. Jump off that dead horse. Otherwise you will wonder "What if?" for the rest of your life. In your golden years, your friends will be Coulda, Shoulda, and Woulda, instead of I Could! I Did! I Tried! I Dared! When you take the risk to be who you are and reach for your dreams, you'll be sharing stories about your adventures. Not what you could or should have done, but your triumphs and failures, mistakes and successes. Take the risk of lifting your feet off the ground, even if you lose your balance once in a while.

Q: If Opportunity Doesn't Knock:

A) Give up

B) Kick the door down

C) Quit your job

D) Ring doorbells

A: You're one smart lady. Yes, D is the answer. Ring every doorbell, even on doors that belong to people you don't know. Network. Meet at least five new people a week. Share your goals, and ask how you can help those you meet reach their goals. Appoint yourself ambassador, and tell everyone you know about your mission. If there is someone you want to meet and they don't have a doorbell, bring them one. Remember, I didn't have tickets to Camelot when I asked out my husband-to-be, but the box office did! Okay, so I rang them by phone—but I rang! You can, too.

Are You On a Dead Horse Quiz

Are you stuck in a dead-end relationship? Sick of the "same old, same old" at work and at home? Perhaps you feel as if you're riding a merry-go-round to nowhere. If your answer is yes, chances are you're riding a Dead Horse. Not sure? Then take this quiz and discover what your score reveals about your situation.

❑ YES ❑ NO   1. Are you settling for less than you deserve in a relationship?

❑ YES ❑ NO   2. Do you complain about work, family or a friend more than three times a day?

❑ YES ❑ NO   3. Has it been more than two years since you changed your hair style?

❑ YES ❑ NO   4. Does guilt set in when you have to say "no" to a family member?

❑ YES ❑ NO   5. Is it easy for you to start an exercise plan but you never stay on it?

❑ YES ❑ NO   6. When it comes to setting personal goals, do you find it easy to procrastinate?

❑ YES ❑ NO   7. Do you feel it's too late to meet your true love?

❑ YES ❑ NO   8. On a daily basis, do you use the words "but", "should've" and "could've"?

❑ YES ❑ NO   9. Even though you are unhappy in your relationship, have you have stayed in it for more than two years?

❑ YES ❑ NO   10. Your partner just wants to be friends but you stay hoping you can change his/her mind?

❑ YES ❑ NO   11. Talking to your mother on the phone stresses you out, but you still call her three times a week or more?

❑ YES ❑ NO   12. Out of boredom, you make three or more personal calls a day from your workplace?

❑ YES ❑ NO   13. Do you feel that things would be different if you had a degree?

❑ YES ❑ NO   14. For more than twenty years, you have been chumming with the same circle of friends?

❑ YES ❑ NO   15. Every job that you've had came along with a boss who was difficult?

❑ YES ❑ NO   16. When you are out socializing, your pride stops you from having fun?

❑ YES ❑ NO   17. When things go wrong, do you have a tendency to blame others?

❑ YES ❑ NO   18. When you fail at something, do you call yourself stupid or other names?

❑ YES ❑ NO   19. The reason you stay in an unhappy situation is because you're afraid of what others might think if you leave?

❑ YES ❑ NO   20. Do you think that your friend has the life you've always dreamed of?

Your Dead Horse Quiz Results!

To calculate your score:
Give yourself ten points for every "yes" answer, then subtract five points for every "no" answer.

Yes _____ x 10 = _____

No _____ x 5 = _____

_____

Your score will fall into one of five categories which will most closely describe your present mindset (dead horse) or the onset of dead horse syndrome (a warning sign that a dead horse is about to adopt you for some time!) There are as many breeds of dead horses as they are women willing to ride them. See page 114 in my book for a list of the most common dead horses.

140 to 200 Denial

You are in definite denial that you're on a dead horse. You are at the starting gate for the run of your life and you're sitting on a dead horse. Think about it. You're unhappy, but you say, "Why change now? I'm doing just fine." You can't possibly win this race if you can't even get out of the starting gate. Your horse is dead! You have been trying to give this horse mouth-to-mouth resuscitation. It is dead. Dismount! You need my book ASAP. The first chapter you should read is Sitting Comfortably In The Saddle Of A Dead Horse.

80 to 140 Passive

You know you are on a dead horse, but hope no one will notice. The race is about to start but some how you think if you smile, sit tall and pretend to be confident no one will notice! You are too fearful, hopeless or insecure to take charge of your own life and change. Please do yourself a favor- get my book and use it for a reference often. I suggest you read the chapter titled Jockey In The Freezer.

20 to 80 Active

OK, so you think you're doing something about it! You keep kicking the dead horse, hoping it will get up and ride again. You have been dressing up the dead horse and taking it out socially for a long time. You have been introducing and complaining about this situation to your friends, co-workers and family. It is dead and the chances of kicking it back to life are nil. Please order my book if not for yourself for the sake of your friends who love you but do not have the courage to tell you that they are tired of hearing about your dead horse. I recommend that you read the chapter about Angie titled If Horses Had Wings!

-40 to 20 Reactive

You never planned to jump off your dead horse but by luck somehow you fell off! Then you climbed right back in the saddle again because it is comfortable; you're used to it. Even though you're unhappy, frustrated or dissatisfied with your life, you are willing to stay on a dead horse. Not if I can help it! Because I know first hand what happiness will occur in your life if you dismount! It's time for you to jump off that dead horse, mount a thoroughbred and blaze a new trail! First get my book and read A Horse With No Sense Of Time!

-100 to -40 Proactive

You're one extraordinary woman who without a doubt will end up in thewinners circle at the run for the roses. You take charge of your life by welcoming change on a daily basis. You are truly an ambassador to all the women who have read my book in hopes of making healthy choices in relationships, finances, the work place and in love by recognizing their dead horses, dismounting and mounting thoroughbreds. For the women in your life who are not as proactive as you, this book would be a wonderful gift!

I'll miss you too but I really have to move on.

List all the reasons to say goodbye to your dead horse:

1 _____

2 _____

3 _____

4 _____

5 _____

6 _____

7 _____

8 _____

9 _____

10 _____

Now Dismount!

Congratulations!
You are on your way!

You can order a personalized
copy of this book by calling (941) 906-2098.
We will gift wrap and ship it for free.

If you want to share a story you think
will help other women dismount
their dead horses, I would love
to hear from you.

www.nodeadhorses.com
(941) 906-2098

Afterword

I hope you've enjoyed this ride, dear ladies, and that you've found the stories of these remarkable women as inspiring as I have. If you know someone who needs it, I hope you'll pass this book along. Or better yet, give her a copy. You may wish to keep this book handy and reread it yourself now and then. Remember, change is the key to personal growth and success. Today's thoroughbreds can become tomorrow's dead horses.

Contact Information

For information about Lynn's seminars or to request her as a keynote speaker for your organization or corporate events, please contact us. Got a story about your own dead horse? We'd love to hear from you!

Lynn McDonald
CESARIO, INC.
1620 Main Street Unit 11
Sarasota, FL 34236
941-906-2098
Fax: 941-362-2003
www.nodeadhorses.com

Sales Information

This book is available at special discounts when purchased in bulk for premiums and sales promotions, as well as for fundraising or educational use.